THE CONSTRUCTION OF SEXUAL AND CULTURAL IDENTITIES

*To my wonderful parents, Neophytos and Meli,
and uncle Glafkos of course*

The Construction of Sexual and Cultural Identities

Greek-Cypriot men in Britain

CONSTANTINOS N. PHELLAS
South Bank University, London, UK

LONDON AND NEW YORK

First published 2002 by Ashgate Publishing

Reissued 2018 by Routledge
2 Park Square, Milton Park, Abingdon, Oxon OX14 4RN
711 Third Avenue, New York, NY 10017, USA

Routledge is an imprint of the Taylor & Francis Group, an informa business

Copyright © Constantinos N. Phellas 2002

The author has asserted his moral right under the Copyright, Designs and Patents Act, 1988, to be identified as the author of this work.

All rights reserved. No part of this book may be reprinted or reproduced or utilised in any form or by any electronic, mechanical, or other means, now known or hereafter invented, including photocopying and recording, or in any information storage or retrieval system, without permission in writing from the publishers.

Notice:
Product or corporate names may be trademarks or registered trademarks, and are used only for identification and explanation without intent to infringe.

Publisher's Note
The publisher has gone to great lengths to ensure the quality of this reprint but points out that some imperfections in the original copies may be apparent.

Disclaimer
The publisher has made every effort to trace copyright holders and welcomes correspondence from those they have been unable to contact.

A Library of Congress record exists under LC control number: 2001099951

ISBN 13: 978-1-138-74254-3 (hbk)
ISBN 13: 978-1-138-74251-2 (pbk)
ISBN 13: 978-1-315-18224-7 (ebk)

Contents

Preface vii
Acknowledgements ix
Author's Note xi

1 Zorba the Gay Greek Man   1

2 Identities, Stigma and the Control of Disclosure   13

3 Three Worlds in Collision   39

4 Cypriot Culture and Homosexuality   57

5 Methodological Issues   73

6 The Gay Greek-Cypriot Man in Britain: A Profile   91

7 Epilogue   115

Appendix   125
Bibliography   133
Index   141

Preface

Attitudes toward sexuality differ within the diverse ethnic and racial communities that exist in Great Britain, and the cultural values and beliefs surrounding sexuality play a major role in determining how individuals behave within their sociological context. The family unit is the domain where such values and beliefs are nurtured and developed. An individual's value system is shaped and reinforced within the family context, which usually reflects the broader community norms. Disclosure of a gay sexual preference and lifestyle by a family member presents challenges to ethnic minority families who tend not to discuss sexuality issues and presume a heterosexual orientation.

For ethnic minority gays the 'coming out' process presents challenges in their identity formation process and in their loyalties to one community over another. Ethnic gay men need to live within three rigidly defined and strongly independent communities: the gay community, the ethnic minority community, and the society at large. While each community provides fundamental needs, serious consequences emerge if such communities were to be visibly integrated and merged. It requires a constant effort to maintain oneself in three different worlds, each of which fails to support significant aspects of a person's life. The complications that arise may inhibit one's ability to adapt and to maximise personal potentials. It has to be emphasised that ethnic minority gay men comprise highly heterogeneous populations, with individuals who make diverse choices in coping, functioning and empowering or disempowering themselves. For example, some ethnic gay men may not turn to their ethnic and cultural traditions for emotional support. However, many ethnic minority gay men will look at some level to a source of comfort and/or nurturing that only their community or family of origin can bring. Indeed, there is no monolithic concept of ethnic minority gay men. What applies to an Anglo-African man does not necessarily apply to a Greek-Cypriot. Similarly, differences exist among men from the same ethnic and racial group. For instance, what applies to an Anglo-Chinese man does not necessarily apply to an Anglo-Japanese man. Furthermore, issues of homophobia vary from culture to culture and within the same ethnic groups.

Coming out is assumed to be an individual process, related to a person's self-concept and identity. It is presumed that acknowledging a lesbian, gay, or bisexual orientation is important to heterosexuals in reducing their homophobia by providing positive role models of gay, lesbian and bisexual people. Failure to acknowledge one's sexual orientation publicly is assumed to represent a form of denial. This is seen as a form of resistance, an indication of self-hatred, shame, embarrassment, or some other negative psychological phenomenon. Many times, coming out is characterised as a dichotomous situation – one is either in or out of the closet – with little notice of what takes place between the two extremes and its sociological and psychological complexity.

The purpose of this book is to examine all the above assumptions that may be salient for white lesbians and gay men but could be very different for the gay Greek-Cypriot men living in Britain. It also explores some issues and raises some questions about coming out as a process that is always embedded in a cultural context that can profoundly shape the experience of that process for individuals. A sample of homosexually/bisexually identified Anglo-Cypriot men was selected and the broad effects of belonging to two marginal and ostensibly antagonistic communities were investigated.

It is suggested that most of the respondents identified more strongly with their gay identities than with their Anglo-Cypriot identities; however, most indicated that acknowledge of both aspects of identity was preferred. Other situational factors, including disclosure of a gay identity to a family and to the Anglo-Cypriot community, as well as discrimination because of sexual orientation, and race, were examined in regard to identity development.

A framework for understanding the process of change that occurs for the gay person as he attempts to resolve conflicts of dual minority membership, is also presented. Finally, future prospects of this research are discussed and also linked to theoretical aspects about identity and sexual orientation.

Acknowledgements

I would like to thank all those people who took part in this research, volunteered information, or offered their ideas and suggestions; and to those who gave their voices, without which this book would never have been completed. The Greek-Cypriot men who took part in this research offered me their time, their voices, and their heart-felt experiences, at times taking the risk of breaking years of silence about matters most important to them. Their voices literally fill many pages of this book. In many important ways, they are the real authors. I hope that this book repays them in the accurate expression of their fears, frustrations and pain, as well as their hopes, aspirations and dreams for the future.

I owe special thanks to the following colleagues and friends for practical and/or intellectual support: ESRC for funding my research, Professor Tony Coxon, Dr Gill Green, Dr Adrian Coyle, Dr Chetan Bhatt, Dr Anton Pozniak, Professor Jeffrey Weeks, Professor John Solomos, Ms Gilly Burrell, Professor Dick Wiggins, Dr Sean Waldron, Dr Faizal Samji, Ms Sarah Fitz-Gerald, Alecos Modinos, Dr Evis Bagdates.

My personal thanks to the following for their unconditional love and friendship: Xander Den Boer ('always in my thoughts and prayers'), John Christie ('Boo Bear and BLTs'), Tao and Reiki ('babies'), Patricia Branley, David Clark, Fay Ostrom, Mariana and Geoff Bayley, Mariam Ibrahim, Dee Chase, Anthea Graves, Julie and Rupert Soskin, Jennifer Johnston, Carlos Moises, Roy John, Ali Birang, Gabriel Koureas, Andreas Wellauer, Glafkos Georgiou, Niki Christodoulou, Paris Sivakas, Andreas Christodoulou, Ian Fraser, Mustafa Atai.

Finally, I want to thank my family (my wonderful parents, Meli and Neophytos and my brother Giorgio) who have shown their unconditional love and support despite the personal challenges I often presented them with.

Author's Note

Firstly, because of the serious and confidential nature of this book, it has been necessary to provide only the first name of the respondents, as well as alter some of the case details, in order to protect the privacy of those concerned from harassment.

Secondly, this book is concerned exclusively with males who have sex with males. Hence although strictly speaking it is not possible *a priori* to determine which of them identify with a gay identity the term 'male homosexual' should be used. However, common usage allows 'homosexual' to be used in its non-gender-marked form (covering males and females), it also allows 'gay' to be used as a synonym for 'male homosexual'. Hence, unless otherwise indicated, this usage will be followed throughout this book. Females who have sex with females are likewise by common usage named as 'lesbians', and this will also be followed.

Chapter 1
Zorba the Gay Greek Man

Introduction

Despite the fact that Cyprus is well known to the British public by virtue of constant media and television advertising and often presented as the Island of Love[1] and a place where the sun always shines, the above respondent makes it clear that those who have never been part of that culture can never really grasp the everyday life ramifications of the Cypriot identity. So far very little research (with the exception of Anthias's book (1992)) has been published on the socio-cultural and economic position of Greek-Cypriots in British society and their development from colonial migrants to a settler population. Very little research is also available in the sociological and psychological literature on how a non-heterosexual Cypriot man or woman living in England forms his or her sexual identity in a cultural context.

The central tenet of Anthias' work is to examine and understand the dynamic interactions and experience of the settler population of Greek-Cypriots within the host country of Britain. Rather than consider ethnicity as a concept, which can be uniformly applied to any given ethnic group, she argues that to understand ethnicity, the internalised socio-cultural characteristics of the group need to be considered within the structural and political processes of the host country. Ethnicity is thus not a unitary concept but is constrained by the divisions of class, gender and ethnic identity and is situationally dependent.[2] This would have implications for sexual identities within ethnic minority groups and more specifically the effect that cultural diversity has on the coming-out process.

The coming out process is defined as the experience of acknowledging a gay, lesbian, or bisexual sexual orientation to oneself and others. In this paradigm, coming out is characterised by a person's development and acceptance of her or his homosexuality and homosexual identity. In the social discourse about coming out, there are many common assumptions that may be of questionable validity but often go unchallenged. One assumption is that the process of coming out is a singular constellation and is dichotomous. That is, a person is either out or not. It is also presumed that acknowledging a gay/lesbian or bisexual sexual orientation, especially to heterosexuals, can reduce the level of homophobia, as it provides others with positive role models of non-stereotypical gay, lesbian, and bisexual people.

Disclosing one's sexual orientation is also thought to be a ubiquitously positive experience that creates self-acceptance and confidence through repeated practice. In fact, for gay men and lesbians, not making public pronouncements about their sexual orientation is presumed to be negative and less than healthy psychologically and is characterised by negative terms, such as living double lives, hiding, being in the closet, and being closeted. Living double lives or being closeted is presumed to indicate shame, denial, and self-hatred. In various forms, these assumptions have found their way into the conceptualisations of research on coming out, development of sexual identities, and homosexuality. Most of these assumptions, however, are based on clinical and empirical studies conducted with white lesbians and gay men. Lesbians and gay men of ethnic minority backgrounds have received scant attention in the sociological and psychological literature on homosexuality and development of sexual identities.

This book attempts to explore some issues and raise some questions about accepting one's homosexuality and subsequently developing a sexual identity as a process that is always embedded in a cultural context that can profoundly shape the experience of that process for individuals.

Developments in Gay and Lesbian Studies

For a century, research on the history of homosexuality has been constrained by the intolerance of governments and academics alike.[3] However, over the last two decades one witnesses an unprecedented outpouring of scholarship in lesbian and gay history pertaining to sexual orientation[4] and about homosexual lives in general. More precisely, we now know more about the experiences of young gay men (Trenchard and Warren, 1984), the old (Berger, 1982), those in prison (Wildeblood, 1957), those who offer sex in exchange for money (Reiss, 1961), and those who lived during particular historical periods (Porter and Weeks, 1991). However, whilst knowledge and awareness about what it means to be gay, lesbian or bisexual in terms of sexual orientation has increased considerably, there remains a deep-seated ignorance on a number of planes. Scientific knowledge about why sexual orientations differ is still scanty despite a number of diverse theories over the past century,[5] and in a society that can still be overtly hostile towards 'deviant' sexual relationships there is still much to learn about the way being attracted to one's own sex, particularly in conjunction with various other co-factors such as occupation can effect self-esteem, the development of personal identity and general cognitive function.

Furthermore, over the years historians have grown more sophisticated in their understanding of sexual ideology and of the relationship between social roles and identity formation. The earliest studies by social constructionists argued that no one who engaged in homosexual behaviour before the last century was labelled – or assumed a distinct identity – as a result of that behaviour because it was considered a sin of which everyone was potentially capable. These studies disagreed primarily about the dating of the emergence of the 'modern homosexual', a distinctive 'type' of person defined on the basis of his or her sexual behaviour and self-identification. Some historians, such as Randolph Trumbach and Alan Bray, dated the appearance of the 'homosexual' from the early eighteenth century, with the appearance of the 'molly houses' in London; others, such as M. Foucault, Jeffrey Weeks and Jonathan Katz placed it at the end of the nineteenth, with the advent of medical inquiry and the further growth of cities.[6]

Ethnic Minorities' Gay Studies – An Unlikely Combination?

What does it mean to be an ethnic minority gay man? For ethnic minority gays, life is often lived in three different communities: the gay community, the ethnic minority community and the predominantly heterosexual white mainstream society. Since these three social groups have their own norms, expectations, and styles, the minority gay man must balance a set of often-conflicting challenges and pressures. The multi-minority status makes it difficult for a person to become integrated and assimilated. Within the mainstream society, ethnic minority gays experience prejudice and discrimination for their ethnic identity, as well as for their sexual orientation. In the gay community the social values mirror those of the mainstream society in relation to their perception of ethnic minorities, which includes negative stereotyping and prejudicial attitudes about ethnic and racial minorities. Hence, ethnic minority gays experience discrimination for their ethnicity within the gay community. In some ethnic minority communities the social norms and values concerning homosexuality foster homophobic attitudes and consequently gays within these minority communities face disapproval and rejection.

Another way to view the lives of ethnic minority gays is to consider them as both a visible and invisible minority. As a visible minority they have no choice but to cope with being the object of racist practices. As an invisible minority they can be discrete about their sexual orientation and hope to minimize the homophobic reactions. Consequently, the communities' racist and homophobic attitudes compromise the potential support they can receive from the three communities. In contrast white gays do not experience racism in the mainstream society. As an invisible minority they can choose to remain silent and not come out or remain invisible. However, the homophobic attitudes of mainstream society and ethnic minority communities limit the support for gays. Thus, remaining invisible usually means suffering in silence.

Goffman (1963) described a process individuals experience as a function of their known identity as a minority. He used the concept of 'discredited' for those who were of a racial or ethnic minority group and 'discreditable' for those who required disclosure in order to be identified as minority. For the 'discredited' the issue is managing the tension generated during social contacts, whereas for the 'discreditable' the issue is managing information about the potential tensions that could be generated if their minority status was disclosed or revealed. The 'discredited' individual must learn coping mechanisms to manage the reactions and interactions from those who discredit. The 'discreditable' individual '... must face unwitting acceptance of himself by individuals who are prejudiced against persons of the kind he can be revealed to be' (Goffman, 1963, p.42). Concealing identity allows for protection from social consequences. Applying this process to ethnic minority gays one can expect the development of a sophisticated decision making process that is central to well functioning coping mechanisms. Social interactions would need to be assigned to either visible or invisible minority status for an appropriate response. In situations where social interactions are viewed as a reaction of dual minority status, managing the tension generated during the social contact would seem to be the response of choice, since the visible or 'discreditable' status is revealed.

It is only relatively recently that Britain has become truly multi-ethnic as the post-war years saw an influx of people from East and West Africa, The Caribbean, India and Pakistan, Cyprus, Eastern European Countries, as well as the more recent growth in numbers from the Far East. Of course cultural divisions have always existed, in the sense that there are markers in the society, which characterise groups of people. Religion, social class, age groups and geography are the more obviously recognisable. Sexual identity and sexual behaviour too can be defined as discriminating characteristics, which can bind and define a culture.

Different cultures set different boundaries and constraints and attach different meanings to sexual behaviour, hence the importance of understanding the cultural context in which sexual behaviour occurs. The comparative study of the dynamics of sexual behaviour may illuminate patterns and processes in Western European cultures hitherto ignored, undetected or seemingly random. For example, the practice in extended families in India of shared households and shared beds among boys provides opportunities for 'play-sex' (*maasti*) and the discharge of sexual tension, without the suggestion of a homosexual identity. While the concept of 'play-sex', for example, is notably absent in Western European and American research literature, it intuitively strikes a familiar chord, and may nevertheless exist, but as a less formalised concept and a considerably more covert practice. Its study may well provide useful insights into the developmental aspects of sexual identity. Behaviour, perhaps ignored in a given culture, can sometimes appear more obviously structured, when viewed in the light of those constructs and motives which are more readily discernible in a comparative culture. Conversely, constructs used to delineate some cultures may be completely absent in others. This is a most important point: conceptual equivalence does not always exist. We may be looking for phenomena from the standpoint of our own experience but which in another culture is simply irrelevant.

Sexual behaviour, its specific expression and the meanings attached to it occur as a function of the culture of which that person is a member. This can be at the macrocosmic level: whether that depends on the culture of his country of origin, the response of his host society, or some new set of dynamics which have arisen in response to his adoptive culture. Or it may exist at the microcosmic level of the city in which he lives or the particular locale visited. What is also evident is that while sexual acts are very similar throughout the world, the cultural meanings and responses to these acts are not universal and can differ markedly. Anthropological and sociological accounts of sexuality in contemporary societies document striking differences in sexual behaviour and the meanings attached to it across different cultural milieus (Caplan, 1987; Whitehead and Ortner, 1981).

While the traditional culture may form a template for a minority ethnic group, the beliefs, values and lifestyles of minority groups do not form a culture, which is a microcosm of their traditional culture. These are unique and constantly evolving and transient systems. It would be naive and utilitarian to presume that a minority ethnic group's culture lies on some continuum between the traditional and the surrounding cultures, although there may be discernible features from both or apparently from neither: it has a character of its own. At the psychosocial level of the individual, each person will have different ways and rates of assimilating into the host culture or remaining separate from it. This again is a reciprocal process that creates its own feedback and change.

The effect of minority ethnic groups' values and behaviours on the host culture must also be acknowledged. It would be reasonable to expect that considerable sexual mixing between men of different ethnic groups will impact upon the dynamics of sexual behaviour and its expression among the various host culture's sub-groups. Minority groups show the same heterogeneity that is evident in any society and it is this inclination to generalise that must be resisted in any minority group research. It is the interrelation of the various aspects of culture that allow us to understand the forms of integration of various types of culture. Relations between the different aspects of culture follow the most diverse patterns and cannot lend themselves profitably to generalisations (Boas, 1932). Only rarely can the relationship between the individual and culture be understood and then at best only indirectly. Each culture's own heterogeneity must be recognised: stereotyping is an easy trap. Generalisations are nevertheless useful and can help to fill in the background, which shapes behaviour, but they are approximations and this should be remembered in any research among any minority groups.

Homosexuality in the Cypriot Culture

Cyprus was till recently the only country member of the Council of Europe, which has not yet abolished the anti-homosexual laws. On 21 May 1998 the Cypriot parliament decided to legalise gay male sex. The vote came eight days before the deadline set by the Council of Europe for Cyprus to end its ban on gay sex or risk being kicked off the Council and barred from entering the European Union. Out of the 56 members of the legislative body, 36 voted for reform, eight against, one abstained and the rest were absent. However, the decision disappointed activists by including clauses banning gay personal ads, prohibiting 'indecent proposals' and attaching higher penalties to gay sexual offences.

The Gay Liberation Movement in Cyprus was founded on 10 December 1987 as an attempt to change the existence of an outdated colonial law. Among the many problems that gay people face in Cyprus are the following:

- Prosecution for criminal behaviour.
- The powerful position of the Greek Orthodox Church which considers homosexual practices 'the gravest of sins'.
- The great social stigma of homosexuality in a culture where family and community play an important role.

The slightest suspicion of homosexuality is enough to make a person an outcast and cause him anxiety, discrimination and unhappiness with the result that homosexuals are forced to conceal their homosexual identity and become invisible. All the members of the Gay Liberation Movement are anonymous except from two people.[7]

However, whilst the subject of homosexuality in the Cypriot culture has been probed, albeit sketchily, almost nothing has been articulated on the direct combination of the two: Homosexuality in the Cypriot culture.[8]

The Starting Point

Instigating a piece of research project is daunting when the only conspicuous starting point is 'the beginning', the literature search revealing less than a handful of directly relevant sources for the work ahead. The only relevant book so far produced is *Omofilofilia*,[9] a collection of papers presented at a conference in Nicosia, Cyprus in 1982. However, despite its relevance it has not been translated into English, making it rather inaccessible. As far as the English language is concerned, it would appear that nothing has been written on the issue of homosexuality in the Cypriot community living in London.

Having consulted the gay Cypriot organisations both in Cyprus and in London this would appear to be the sum total of work in the area, excepting an assortment popular articles published by journalists in Cyprus and of the community here, on the gay groups that now exist. The next of kin, and only close relation in the domain, is the work done on other ethnic minority communities as described in section above.

Furthermore, there is a narrow literature on the Cypriot migration within current developments in the field of 'race' and ethnic studies (George and Millerson, 1967; Constantinides, 1977; Ladbury, 1977; Anthias, 1992).[10]

Research Objectives

Introduction

This book concerns sexual identity formation in the context of a bicultural background in which one of the cultures is non-Western. (The term non-Western is used to signify the difference in the way Cypriot culture views issues of sexuality and homosexuality from the typical Western Anglo-American one.) Much contemporary thinking about identity comes from psychology, anthropology, sociology, and more recently, cultural studies and focuses on identity as a self-definition and as a social construction. Theoretical models of sexual identity development have come from a Western tradition and have not accounted for cultural differences in approaches to sexuality (including sexual expression) and sexual identity. It is inaccurate to generalise about people of colour as a homogeneous group, or to group non-Western cultures together; however, the issues addressed in this book, focusing on one bicultural group of Anglo-Cypriots, may apply to other ethnic minority groups.

Since so little research has been done on the issue of sexual identity and sexuality in a non-Western cultural context, this book raises questions which can be addressed by social scientists and cultural historians in pursuit of understanding sexual identity formation. It also summarises the historical background of the development of the concept of sexual identity in the West and examines psychological and sociological models of homosexual/ethnic minority identity development.

Exploring cultural differences in sexual expression, sexuality, and sexual identity for Anglo-Cypriots and other ethnic minority groups, it also raises questions to be addressed in future research. Although identity is a fluid concept in psychological and sociological terms, we tend to speak of fixed identities. In particular, those aspects of identity, which characterise observable physical characteristics, such as race or gender, are viewed as unchanging ascribed identities. Examples of these include identifications such as a Cypriot woman or an Anglo-Cypriot man, or even broader terms such as woman of colour and man of colour. These constructions of identity are based on physical appearance and an individual's declaration of identity. However, even these seemingly clear distinctions are not definitive. In the context of identities based on racial and physical characteristics, ascribed identities will, rightly or wrongly, continue to be attributed to individuals by others. It is left up to the individual to assert personal identity and demonstrate it to others.

The definition of sexual identity is more ambiguous still, whether taken as a concept by itself or in context with cultural, racial, ethnic, or gendered identities. With sexual identity, it is generally those individuals who are considered 'sexual minorities', such as lesbians, gay men, and bisexual persons, who define and declare their sexual identities. Unless there is a specific focus on sexual orientation, few in the 'majority' self-consciously identify as heterosexuals. Given the assumption of heterosexuality in the Western societies, acknowledging a sexual identity is an inherently political statement.

Even if it is one identity among several, and it is not given priority over racial, ethnic, or gendered identities, individuals who declare a non-majority sexual identity become identified primarily in terms of this sexual identity. It is because of this 'primary effect' of transgressive sexual identity that lesbians, gay men, and bisexuals of colour may be reluctant to take on a sexual identity. A declaration of lesbian/gay/bisexual identity can overshadow their racial/ethnic identity, and the latter identity generally affords a powerful sense of social belonging and group affiliation.

Cultural background plays an important role in determining how an individual integrates sexuality into his or her sense of identity. Non-Western cultures such as the Cypriot culture do not have the same concept of sexual identity as the European-American tradition. The models of sexual identity development and the paradigms of identity for the individual self may not be applicable for individuals who have non-Western cultural backgrounds. Indeed, one can ask whether Western sexual identity paradigms are applicable to people of colour at all. Some researchers have already questioned whether the categories of sexual identity and sexual behaviour are accurate in describing people of colour, noting that black and Hispanic men who are categorised as 'homosexual' or 'bisexual' by Westerns do not necessarily identify themselves as such (Alonso and Koreck, 1993; Hammonds, 1987; Morales, 1989; Worth and Rodriguez, 1987). Anthropologists Alonso and Koreck (1993) note that:

> Anglo-American sexual distinctions – 'heterosexual', 'bisexual', and 'homosexual' –, which have been reified ..., are neither universal nor natural but instead socio-culturally and historically produced categories, which cannot be presumed to be applicable to Anglo/American minority groups or to other societies. (p.114)

It can be argued that minority ethnic groups living in the UK (particularly second or even third generation nationals) exhibit different social characteristics from those in the country of origin. This is undoubtedly true. In fact, Diaspora communities are frequently observed to show greater conservatism and resistance to change with rigid adherence to maintaining traditional customs and practices. This is particularly evident when the ethnic minority group is largely composed of people from peasant societies, who share many common features, regardless of whether the group is Cypriot, Indian, Pakistani, Polish, Italian, Jewish etc. Among Afro-Caribbeans the background of plantation economy coupled with slavery impacted uniquely on the rural peoples and their resultant cultures.

It is important and instructive to contemplate the origins and dynamics of the underlying social values of the Cypriot ethnic minority group, which is the foci of this study, so that an understanding is reached of the context in which, sexual behaviour occurs among ethnic minorities who are no longer resident in their country of origin. Without this background study there are no pegs on which to hang any subsequent theorising, and no framework to guide our understanding of current sexual practices. When viewed in this way, it becomes vital.

An individual's social values and expectations are generally derived from family systems, which tend to reflect the broader community mores and it is their impact on identity and sexual identity, which needs to be considered. These first and second generation immigrant men's attitudes and behaviour will be affected by the retention of some of the values and traditions of their country of origin. The prescription of gender role expectations and the sanctioning of certain sexual behaviours will affect the extent to which an individual is able to openly identify as 'gay'. This presents important implications for disclosure of identity, for perceived risk for HIV infection and acceptance or denial of that risk.

The term 'family' is used in its widest anthropological sense and describes systems of nurturing and caring of offspring. The Western notion of nuclear family is an appropriate model from which to regard cultures rooted in similarly derived cultures, but it would be restrictive to employ this concept to ethnic minority groups, whose familiar systems are often based on more extended groups, which may not necessarily include blood relations.

The research objectives It would seem then that this book, in addressing the notion of homosexuality in the Cypriot culture, does so academically for the first time in this country, and as such, there has been no solid foundation of prior work to build on, hence, the basic research aims are several. Firstly, there is an attempt to address a number of rudimentary questions regarding the non-heterosexual Cypriot man living in London. Nine main questions are highlighted for investigation:

- Activism and participation in the Anglo-Cypriot and gay communities.
- Choice of community (Anglo-Cypriot versus gay) in which individuals felt more comfortable.
- Self-definition of identity.
- Disclosure or nondisclosure of gay identity to their families.
- What are the effects of the 'double life syndrome' on i) the general psychological well-being of the Anglo-Cypriot men, ii) their ability to form and maintain personal relationships.
- How do gay Anglo-Cypriot men negotiate a path through their two worlds to avoid their coming into conflict, and what is the result when they meet?
- Cypriot cultural factors in acceptance of gayness.
- Perceptions of gay Anglo-Cypriots by the gay community, the Cypriot community, and the mainstream English society.
- Perceptions of discrimination because they are gay or Anglo-Cypriots or because they are both gay and Anglo-Cypriots.

Finally, a framework will be presented which can be used to examine sexual expression and the formation of a sexual identity for people of colour within the specificity of a particular ethnic group's cultural norms and values. Since sexuality is related to the meanings given to erotic feelings and actions in a specific culture, the range of sexual behaviours which are considered acceptable, the forms of sexual expression, who may express which forms of sexuality, as well as what is perceived as deviation are all factors that must be considered in understanding the formation of sexual identity (Greene, 1994).

The Research Population: 'Gay Cypriots'

The investigation of the 'double life' syndrome is one, which, due to its inherent nature, is difficult to research. For the purpose of this research, the observation and network tracing[11] together with the contact advertisements were considered to be the most suitable and preferred methods for selecting my sample. This is due to the fact that sub-groups like the Cypriot one are often 'doubly invisible' combining homosexual behaviour with other characteristics such as heterosexual marriage or ethnic status which make them hard-to-reach. There already exists a Cypriot Lesbian and Gay Group (CLGG) in London, which has close links with the Gay Movement in Cyprus. Membership, however, of both groups is low.

Potential sources for sample recruitment include:

- Members of the Cypriot Gay and Lesbian Group.
- Various GUM clinics based in North and South London where the majority of the Cypriot community resides.
- Telephone contacts.
- Gay organisations that happen to have any Cypriot members.
- Personal advertisements in the local community paper.
- Personal contacts through network tracing.

The overall difficulty of all the above is that of access and of distortion towards the overt as opposed to covert sexualities. For the purpose of this research, the following methods were thought of as potential solutions, or at least palliative, to these issues:

- Use of snowball sampling as this potentially builds trust, breaks down barriers of access and ultimately forms some cohesiveness in the sample, the problem is that it is limited to repetitions of the same type of people and may often dry up.
- Use of informants and contacts to which the same criteria mostly apply.
- Use of personal advertisements in the gay press; and lastly.
- Use of self-disclosure and validation as ways of gaining trust.

The means of sampling and recruitment ultimately employed, included: firstly, the use of snowball sampling from formal and informal contacts; secondly, writing to gay groups and organisations; and thirdly advertising in the gay press. In the end, twenty-two interviews were conducted (n=22) between January and November 1995 and the details of these are given in the interview schedule in note three.

Conclusion

The remaining chapters will examine some features of both the Cypriot and the gay cultures in an attempt to more readily locate the real dilemma of the non-heterosexual Cypriot man, the consequences of the two cultures in conjunction with each other will also be considered and the final part of part one will be devoted by looking at the way the Cypriot culture views homosexuality and indeed sexuality. Also where appropriate extracts from the interviews will be presented to illustrate the argument. In part two, the background to the research is outlined and discussed and also the current research data is both appraised and analysed.

Notes

1   Channel 4, after 10 p.m. advertisement based on the slogan 'Fall in love with Cyprus – the island of Venus'; March to April 1996.
2   Furthermore, Anthias argues that the booming economy of Britain in the 1950s and 1960s attracted migrant labour from many colonial countries and Greek-Cypriots constituted one such ethnic minority. A common characteristic of migrant groups is a disadvantage in terms of their access to the economic opportunities of the host community. Occupational choice and employment are not simply an outcome of the cultural characteristics of the ethnic group, but is also a product of ethnic disadvantage and exclusion due to the sectarian and ethnic dominance of the British society. Greek-Cypriots are also marginalised because discussions concerning racism do not embrace the Greek-Cypriot culture, despite the link between the development of racism within capitalist economies and the development of colonial relations.

The first generation of Cypriot immigrants came primarily from depopulated rural areas, their lives involving not only immigration but also a transition into an urban economy. With low language skills and low educational and occupational qualifications, the occupational opportunities for this first generation were clearly constrained. Women's skills in cooking and sewing became a resource for employment in catering, clothing and retail industries and these, in turn, relied on family employment.

It is a continuing characteristic of the Greek-Cypriot community today that provides a high level of employment and mutual services within the ethnic population. Greek-Cypriots retain a distinctive cultural identity with their own economic and community structures, and geographically high concentrations of the population are located in particular areas of London. The continuance of this strong ethnic identity in the face of increasing access and involvement in educational and occupational structures of the host society is testament to the role of family and community in the construction of individual identities.
3   See for example John Addington Symonds, the nineteenth-century British classicist and arguably the first modern historian of homosexuality, who dared print only ten copies of his study of Greek homosexuality, *A Problem in Greek Ethics*. Secondly, in Berlin Magnus Hirschfeld and other German homosexual intellectuals who have founded the Institute for Sex Research in 1919 witnessed their entire research work destroyed in 1933 in the first major book burning organised by the Nazis. In the USA Cold War-era scholars ignored the

researchers who dared launching the ONE institute for Homophile Studies in Los Angeles in the mid-1950s.

4   See McIntosh, 1968; Humphreys, 1970; Plummer, 1975; Foucault, 1980; Weeks, 1985; Altman, 1989; Greenberg, 1990.
5   See the work done by Ulrichs, 1825–1895; Krafft-Ebing, 1886; Hirschfeld, 1914; Ellis, 1896; Freud, 1905; Dorner, 1975.
6   Randolph Trumbach, 'London's Sodomites: Homosexual Behaviour and Western Culture in the Eighteenth Century', *Journal of Social History* 11 (1977), pp.1–33; Alan Bray, *Homosexuality in Renaissance England* (London, 1982); Jeffrey Weeks, *Coming Out: Homosexual Politics in Britain from the Nineteenth Century to the Present* (London, 1977)
7   One of which is the founder member and president of the Gay Liberation Movement, namely Alexander Fotis Modinos.
8   The only time that the subject of homosexuality was touched upon was in 1982 when a conference organised by the National Organisation of Psychologists discussed the socio and cultural issues of homosexuality.
9   'Omofilofilia, Omilies ke sizitisis pou eyinan sto seminario', *I Omofilofilia*, 20–21 Martiou 1982.
10 Most probably the most up to date piece of research on this area. Anthias' book provides an account of the economic and social position of Cypriots in British society paying particular attention to a number of central theoretical and political debates relating to class, ethnicity, cultural identity, racism, gender and immigration. Her data was collected by the method of participant observation between 1980 and 1982 and subsequently 1988–1990.
11 See Chapter 5 for the initial contacts that took place in the Summer/Autumn 1994. Also a list of groups and organisations is provided asking them for interview volunteers. Additionally, copies of my advertisement were sent to the perspective managers of these organisations for distribution.

   An advertisement for volunteers (Summer/Autumn 1994) was placed in *Capital Gay* for one month, in *Gay Times* for three months and *Boyz* for one month. Also it appeared in the local community paper *Pariaki*.

Chapter 2

Identities, Stigma and the Control of Disclosure

Introduction

Identity is not a fixed entity. It is a complex, interactive and developmental process. For the purposes of this chapter, identity is defined as a complex constructive process of self-definition in interaction with the wider social, economical and political context. Consequently, definitions of sexual identity have altered over the last century and particularly since the political development of a positive 'gay' as opposed to 'homosexual' identity in the late 1960s and early 1970s. Consequently, in contemporary society, identity is particularly important to at least some people in minority, stigmatised and or oppressed groups. For example, to say, 'I am black' or 'I am gay' potentially implies a sense of personal oppression or political opposition. It is important to point out, though, that this does not explain the personal or individual development of identity. Thus, on top of this political context of identity, there is the study of the development of identity, which tends to fall into three primary perspectives:

Firstly, psychoanalysis, where a prior 'polymorphous perversity' is seen to develop into a single sexual orientation;

Secondly, sex role theories where sexuality is seen as culturally and historically contingent and constituted in acts not identities; and

Thirdly, interactionism where sexuality is primarily seen as an identity construct developing interactively out of a specific cultural and historical context.

The difficulty with all of these perspectives though is that they are mostly too simplistic and too linear (often based on sequence/stage theories) as models of development to completely explore or explain the vast complexities of individual, or even collective, experience. A person's difficulty in accepting and acknowledging their sexuality as exclusively heterosexual is associated usually with the problems arising from the following three factors: a) the formation of a working non-heterosexual identity, b) the control of information disclosure and the management of stigma, and c) the process known as 'coming out'. This particular chapter will consider the development of identity, and particularly sexuality and gendered identity, in relation to a study of the interview data I have collected. Furthermore, the other two sections will be examined in the light of the interviews' material. Finally, the role of Queer Theory and Identity will be discussed.

The Formulation of Non-Heterosexual Identity

Troiden (1988) defines identity as:

> ... a cognitive construct referring to organised sets of characteristics that an individual perceives as representing the self definitely in relation to a social situation, imagined or real. (p.27)

The word 'identity' is derived from the Latin *idem*, which means 'the same thing'. As a result when referring to a person's identity, we refer then, to a 'person's essential continuous self; the internal, subjective concept of oneself as an individual' (Reber, 1985). Identities are constructs that individuals create for themselves. As DuBay (1987) has remarked: 'you are only gay when you decide that you are' (p.2). Two types of identity may be postulated for each self: The first might be termed 'private identity' and is the person as he believes himself to be. The second might be termed 'public identity' and is the person as he projects himself to be when dealing with others. There may or may not be a disparity between these two identities. 'Sexual identity' is a more complicated affair and takes a different dimension than the above two discussed.

The very idea of sexual identity can be ambiguous and complex. In the Western world, it has become a concept of absolute importance as more and more sexually marginal people claim a slice from the notion 'sexual identity'. It has often taken priority over other identities to the extent that how we see ourselves sexually is more important than class, racial, or professional loyalties. Statements such as 'I am gay', 'I am lesbian', 'I am into S&M', or 'I am bisexual' are more than mere statements of sexualities. They are statements about belonging, which are offering a sense of personal unity and social location. Additionally, they are at times statements of political commitment as they take a specific stance in relationship to the dominant sexual codes.

Weeks (1988) argue that there is a real paradox at the heart of the question of sexual identity. On the one hand, people become increasingly aware on a theoretical, historical or even on a political level that 'sexuality' is about flux and change and yet they constantly strive to fix it, stabilise it, say who they are by telling of their sex. It seems as Gallop (1982, p.xii) has put it, that:

> ... identity must be continually assumed and immediately called into question; or alternatively constantly questioned yet all the time assumed. For it is provisional, precarious, dependent on, and increasingly challenged by social contingencies and psychic demands – but apparently necessary, the foundation stone of our sexual beliefs and behaviours.

Avoiding the Homosexual Role

Researchers over the years have been trying to explain the different ways in which men and women come to adopt what has become to be known (McIntosh, 1968) the 'homosexual role', and a role, which frequently dominates, and controls the identities of those concerned. Additionally, they have been trying to study the large number of men and women who experience homosexual relationships but manage to avoid adopting the role and the acquisition of a homosexual identity. Both questions are interrelated and interconnected. In the following paragraphs I will try and deal with the latter one and attempt to identify some of the methods used to avoid the acquisition of a homosexual identity and the stigma that typically accompanies it.

As Weinberg (1971) points out, the acknowledgment of homoerotic feelings has frequently been identified as fundamental in the formation of lesbian/gay identities. As a result of that, people feel they have homosexual tendencies may be eager to denounce them in order to avoid the pursuing homosexual identity. Males in particular, perhaps, feel that in the acceptance of their homo desires, they will disturb the stability of their heterosexual masculinity and become something of a congenitally maladjusted or 'perverse' type of person, with an inverted or mixed-up gender make-up.

For over a hundred years now scientific and popular belief has often held that male homosexuality derives from and expresses something 'feminine' in men – the absence of appropriate levels of masculinity. To be homosexual and 'normal' are two things incompatible and cannot represent a realistic presentation of oneself within the general heterosexual context. As a result of that the homosexual identity has been perceived as a product of those institutionalised medical discourses that have dominated the modern Western thinking in sexuality. But the popular belief is so far removed from the truth as it is easy to point to times and places, ancient and modern, where homosexual desire accompanies conventional manliness, heterosexual desire, and very specific relations restricted to particular men (Segal, 1993).

However, the real problems begin here as the individuals receive conflicting messages about their sexuality: their attraction to their own sex clashes with the unrealistic presentation (of those feelings) by the heterosexual population they live in. The dilemma they face is big as they struggle to unlearn or deconstruct what has been passed over to them over the years. For a lot of them the quest to demystify the accepted notion of the homosexual stereotype and start learning to see themselves according to their own meanings and definitions is a huge task to undertake. Subsequently they choose to dismiss the idea of being gay/lesbian altogether, and simply learn to live with their feelings and emotions. They tend to believe that no one else is sharing a similar experience. Over the years researchers have attempted to describe various methods of 'neutralising' self-labelling as 'deviant' (see for example Sykes and Matza (1957); Mills (1974); Marshall (1981)). Hecken (1984) describes some of the most popular ways of presenting or 'window-dressing' a homosexual identity. The following six explanations are among them:

- **Just a Phase**
  The notion of a phase is a common one, which may be, used either retrospectively or in the present. This construction allows the individual to maintain and protect his notion of heterosexual masculinity by distancing himself from the opposing category – that of the homosexual.

- **Just Feeling Horny**
  Here, the individual tries to justify his homosexual behaviour by the 'just feeling horny' excuse. Again, any homosexual feeling is denied – the sexual object is only contingently male – and only the most basic pleasure is derived. Others might argue that they were simply experimenting or were curious. However, those whose experimentation period lasts beyond the 'one night stand' affair may develop a philosophy, which stresses the advantages of the sexual variety in one's life. Furthermore, some of them would argue that sex with men is more readily available and without commitment – where no commitment often equals 'no real homosexual feelings'.

- **Seduction**
  In this case the person may claim that it was not his fault but he has been seduced, perhaps when drunk. Again, the implication is that without the seducer the said behaviour would not have occurred. This scenario frees the person from any responsibility and allows him to enjoy the pleasure without guilt.

- **Situational Homosexuality**
  In some cases (e.g. prison, boarding school) a homosexual outlet may be the only sexual outlet available. However, the individual might argue that in such circumstances the fantasy (if any), which accompanied the act, was a heterosexual one and hence his heterosexual identity remains intact.

- **Sex for Money**
  As Reiss (1961) has pointed out a lot of the sex workers claim to be heterosexual. They are reported to maintain that the only incentive when engaging in homosexual behaviour is a monetary one hence their behaviour is restricted to certain acts. Furthermore, they might strongly deny any homosexual emotional attachment, indeed, there may even be a claim of revulsion.

- **The 'Completely Drunk' Syndrome**
  This is yet another popular method of avoiding the homosexual stigma, allowing the person to enjoy a homosexual behaviour through a claim of temporary alcoholic amnesia.

Throughout all the above scenarios, the individual is struggling to reconcile his 'ideal self' – what he would like to be, and his 'real self' – what he knows himself to be (self-concept) (Atchley, 1982). In his attempts to achieve the above he might experience a low self-esteem feeling and levels of anxiety. A possible (partial) solution that is applied to some of the problems of same-sex attraction is that of a bisexual identity. However, often it creates more problems that it is supposed to resolve as bisexuality consists of a mingling of sexual feelings, behaviours, and romantic inclinations that does not easily gel with society's categories of typical sexuality.

As Blumstein and Schwartz (1977) point out:

> The implications of viewing human sexuality as being plastic and malleable have never been exploited. Even the word bisexuality gives a misleading sense of fixedness to sex-object choice, suggesting as it does a person in the middle, equidistant from heterosexuality and from homosexuality, equally erotically disposed to one gender or the other. (p.44)

Thus, many bisexuals are forced to make a choice between homosexuality and heterosexuality because of the pressures put upon them by society. However, even if not homophobic themselves, many have difficulty accepting the label homosexual in their lives because of its negative image. They feel confused about the homosexual label and what it connotes as they are constantly exposed to negative stereotypes of homosexuals (e.g. queers, fags, sick, queens) by the mainstream heterosexual population.

Deprogramming

Cass (1979) points out that the engagement of positive role models is frequently responsible for allowing the arduous processes of deprogramming and the reconstruction of an affirmative identity. However, the lack of such models in our society means that for many, this process can be delayed for years. Usually, the individual goes through a number of stages before he acquires a positive homosexual identity. These stages will be examined in more detail shortly. In some cases, if the 'scene' is not discovered at all or the newcomer finds himself totally disenchanted by what they find, then the transition may be deferred – indeed in some cases the deferment may prove to be permanent, with the individual returning to earlier coping strategies (Cass, 1979).

As one of my interviewees said:

> I always thought if I met a gay person I would bond with them instantly at that age. I thought if they are gay they will understand about persecution and hassle, they won't be racist, they won't be sexist. I used to meet gay people and have very high expectations of them and then they would say something really racist or really misogynistic. The whole thing made me cynical and sad about gay people and the gay scene. I've realised that there is no silver lining on this cloud. As a matter of fact I didn't want to do anything with gay people for a long time. (Kenan)

Accepting the Homosexual Role

McIntosh (1968) in her classic article 'The Homosexual Role', pointing to the historical and cultural specificity of the 'homosexual', argues that we should recognise that in the current Western context we are dealing with a constructed rather than what came to be seen as a fixed medical or psychiatric category. It is a category defined not simply or exclusively in terms of actual behaviour, but in terms of the social ideas and expectations surrounding any manifestation of same-sex erotic desire. For male homosexual behaviour, these expectations involve an anticipated general effeminacy, sexual desire exclusively for men, and sexual desire aroused in all encounters with any men – but particularly boys and young men. (This contrasts with other times and places, ancient and modern, where homosexual desire accompanies conventional manliness and heterosexual desire.)

We now turn to the question: How is it that so many men do come to adopt gay identities? Many people, it has been argued, 'drift' into identity, battered by contingency rather than guided by choice or preference. Some choices are forced on individuals, whether through stigmatisation and public obloquy or through political necessity. As Kinsey (1948) noted,

> One of the factors that materially contributes to the development of exclusively homosexual histories, is the ostracism which society imposes upon one who is discovered to have had perhaps no more than a lone experience. (p.663)

Writers such as Mead (1928); McIntosh (1968); Plummer (1975); Foucault (1978); Trumbach (1977, 1985); Herdt (1981); Weeks (1981, 1985) and others have through their work made the historical and cultural preconditions of sexual identity abundantly clear. But what needs to be addressed is that such important preconditions cannot only be held responsible for the process of homosexual self-identification. Identity is a choice and cannot be dictated by internal imperatives. As Plummer (1975) argues from a symbolic interactionism perspective, sexual ideas and meanings are constructed in from social interaction with others and then shape people's self-perception and developing identities. 'Self-indication' and 'self-reaction', then, may be just as analytically important as societal reactions' (Plummer, 1975).

Sexual identity theorists use the following two paradigms as part of the theoretical perspective in the essentialist/constructionist debate: the 'sexual orientation' model and the 'identity construct' model. It is not the purpose of this chapter to expand on the complications arising from this debate. However, I would agree with Weeks (1991) who argues that although this debate has been useful, the dichotomy has become increasingly 'polemical', 'arid', and is one which has led to a good degree of 'false polarisation' (pp.86, 6).

The broad theoretical differences in the above models are as follows: Those who support the orientation model, whilst disagreeing on the causes, believe that a person's sexual orientation is established before puberty, possibly as a result of some biological genetic disposition. Furthermore, the establishment is permanent and represents a 'true' sexual core, from which, the sexual identity of the individual emerges at puberty along with the simultaneous realisation of a particular, pre-pubescently constructed, sexual orientation. In most cases, the orientation will complement the identity though this need not always be the case. It would, for example, be possible through conditioning for a person to develop a heterosexual identity, in spite of their homosexual behaviour.

The identity construct view, takes a different stance. Here, it is assumed that a person's identity is formed through an ongoing cognitive and interactive process whereby a person constantly evaluates their emotional and behavioural history and uses this to build an identity. Identity is '... striven for, contested and negotiated'. (Weeks, 1991, p.94). One advantage of this approach over the orientation model is that it allows time for the formation of the 'appropriate' identity after orientation is discovered. This is critical since regardless of whether or not one accepts that orientation is established by puberty, it does not follow that a person's identity is similarly formed. The former in no way compels the latter and any model making such an assumption is likely to prove too inflexible to explain the many years it often takes homosexuals who are aware of their orientation to form homosexual or bisexual identities, or why many men are able to engage in homosexual activity for large portions of their lives without ever establishing gay or bisexual identities.

The 'Ideal-Typical' Model of Identity Formation

Over the last two decades, various researchers have attempted to describe the development and formation of the 'homosexual identity' through a number of theoretical models (e.g. Cass, 1979, 1984; Hammersmith and Weinberg, 1973; Plummer, 1975; Blumstein and Schwartz, 1975; Troiden, 1979, 1980, 1988; Weinberg, 1978, 1983; Ponse, 1978; Minton and McDonald, 1984 and Sophie 1986). Troiden (1988) has identified the following similarities among these models:

- The strong negative connotation that is attached to the homosexual identity by the mainstream heterosexual population.
- That a gay identity before fully developed is subject to a series of conflicts.
- The gradual acceptance of the word 'homosexual' as a label referring to one's self.
- The 'coming out' process is characterised by the gradual desire of the individual to come out to others.

Troiden then proceeds to combine his earlier model with a number of the above-mentioned approaches to arrive at the following 'Ideal – Typical' model, which is considered below:

Sensitisation This stage takes place during childhood where the individual becomes aware of the possibility of being different to his or her peers. This point came up during my interviews and comments like the following were common:

> Even as young as seven I remember not having sexual attraction but finding the male species more appealing to me. (Andreas)

Andrew (his first realisation was at school) also said:

> Well, what was happening was that during the breaks, when we would go into the playground and play, there was this guy that was about ten, and everybody else would play with their friends in the class, and I would always go with him and we'd always play together. And I felt something for him then, at that age. (Andrew)

Research also by Bell, Weinberg and Hammersmith (1981) showed that homosexual males were almost twice as likely as their heterosexual counterparts to report feeling 'very much' or 'somewhat' different from other boys.

For example:

> No, I didn't have any sexual feelings at the age of ten but I knew that something was happening. I knew that I was different from the other lads. I knew there was something going on there. When my friend gave me the chance it just happened. (Lou)

However, one should be careful when dealing with issues of reconstructing the past in search for one's sexual identity aetiology. It may be the case that individuals might have felt 'different' only when asked to go back to their childhood and reconstruct events that might explain their homosexuality. Loftus and Palmer (1974) and Piaget (1962) have done some work on 'constructive memory' and recollection of important childhood events which never occurred). Troiden, although he does not explain to us why this should be so, believes that the sensitisation stage is a necessary (but not sufficient) condition for the subsequent development of a gay identity.

Identity confusion This stage occurs during adolescence and it represents the realisation that the person is engaging in homosexual behaviour and that they may be homosexual. 'It is often characterised by an inner turmoil and uncertainty surrounds their ambiguous sexual status' (Troiden, 1988, p.45). This is a result of the individual entering the stage of 'marginal consciousness' (see later chapters) where he realises that his homosexual tendencies are regarded by the majority as a deviant form of sexual expression. It may be the case that prior to that realisation the individual has been involved into same-sex activities but nevertheless he has been assuming that he was 'normal', i.e. heterosexual. It may therefore take some time before it dawns on him that the nature of his activities are being considered similar to many other types of 'sinful' and 'depraved' sexual practices which are 'against nature'. Troiden suggests that the age around one comes to perceive himself as homosexual is seventeen (eighteen in the case of lesbians). This is despite the fact that by the age of nineteen, most of these committed lesbians and gay males of the future have already experienced sexual activity with both sexes (Bell, Wienberg and Hammersmith, 1981). Troiden carries on to identify a number of strategies as being used in dealing with identity confusion. They have as follows:

a) The physical attack or sending up of homosexuals.
b) 'Repair', is a strategy where the individual attempts to 'exorcise' his homoerotic feelings through the use of 'professional' methods such as those used in psychiatry etc.
c) 'Escapism', is a strategy where alcohol and drugs are used as a form of temporary relief.
d) 'Avoidance' allows the individual to spend more time with the opposite sex (heterosexual 'immersion') thereby sidestepping the problem, or by avoiding any contact with material of any sexual nature that might trigger of sexual feelings.

Andreas was struggling between his religious upbringing and sexual feelings, and commented:

> Oh yes, definitely. In fact I felt guilty from the very onset until I was mature and understood. But the society didn't recognise what I was up to. It wasn't normal, so to speak. But in addition to that, the biggest factor that induced guilt in me was the religious aspect and it ran very strong in my family. While I was in Cyprus, I was quite a religious person. I used to go to church very frequently, I used to be the priest's assistant basically. So, I saw my sexual tendencies as being in disunity with the religious teachings. So, it did bother me a lot. It still bothers me, but not as much as it used to bother me. (Andreas)

Some others turned to religion to find a cure for their homosexuality:

> I was very, very young. I was nine, ten, very young, very young. I didn't actually do anything about it until I was twenty-one, because I suppressed it for that long. I actually went to a friend of mine who's a Christian, who told me to go to this place in France called Lourdes to heal myself, to cure myself of my 'perversion'. So, I went and I wasn't cured, put it that way. (Kostas)

In some cases, the help of a counsellor or a psychiatrist was asked to help them understand their feelings:

> In the last five years, or about five years ago, I spoke to a psychiatrist about it in London and I said 'Look, I've been experiencing emotional problems about myself. There are reasons about how I feel', and I gave him the whole scenario of my life, basically from day one. He's a qualified psychiatrist. He was able to give me a number of explanations, or the mere fact that he just listened to what I had to say and had a professional opinion about the whole thing made me feel less guilty and less remote. I think he helped to shed some light into my emotional problems. (Andreas)

Mike also stated:

> Yes, I did have a nervous breakdown a couple of times. Two or three, perhaps more than that, not in the classical sense of being delirious, but it could be classed like that, yes. (Mike)

Others have chosen to abstain completely from any sexual encounter hoping that the confusion and turmoil would just go way. George reflected:

> Well then, I just became a completely non-sexual being for the next ten years. Out of choice and guilt. Guilt rather than choice. Guilt. Basically, I spent the next ten years denying what I know was reality, really, and pretending to myself that I could try and be straight, that I should have girl-friends. (George)

Another interviewee, Georgis, also commented:

> But I did feel very depressed a lot of the time and very lonely, very, very lonely, I mean, incredibly lonely. (George)

Similarly, John, added:

> I think I felt frightened more than anything. First of all I was confused because everyone all around you, you get all these different signals and you're feeling something totally different and frightened because you don't know anybody else who felt the same. (John)

He went on to say:

> Yes. I was very frightened because there was no one else I could talk to and all the proper ways of growing up were going on all around, blokes getting interested in girls and you were almost forced to fit in with that and I just felt very uncomfortable about all of it. (John)

In some cases, the individual had to face bullying from his schoolmates if he was unfortunate enough to be picked on. Nick said:

> I felt terrified because I was so aware of being different and I became more and more aware and very conscious that I stayed away from boys. I mean, they just absolutely terrified me. I think, very often in that period at school, boys understood my vulnerability and capitalised on it. So that boys, I think, straight boys, who knew I was gay, would kind of try and get their rocks off by getting me to make love and I wouldn't So, it was a kind of hiding my sexuality from people, and it was my great fear that people would find out, up until I was seventeen. (Nick)

Definitions of sexual identity are linked to gendered identity as one added factor is the fact that the definition of homosexuality was frequently linked to a feeling of or identification with femininity, which then extended the self-definition of sexuality to more than sexuality. Kadir, one of the first interviewees, said:

I mean I wasn't like the other boys; I didn't like going out and playing rough games with boys. I was a lonely child most of the time. I preferred the company of girls and playing with dolls and so on. (Kadir)

Identity assumption During this stage there is an increased commitment to homosexual identity and the process of contacting other homosexuals to counter the isolation and alienation begins.

Usually, the place of work provided a safe place for the individual to express and acknowledge his sexual identity.

George said:

It was when I was on my Theatre Design course that I decided that enough was enough and that I was never going to feel less guilty about it. I would just have to do it and just get on with it, become a real person again, you know. I was fed up with sitting at home and being alone and lonely and pretending. Well, at that point, it felt that I was entering such a dark, unknown world. Coming out was basically such a hard thing to do because I thought, I was going, like everyone else does, to lose every single friend I had. No one was going to talk to me ever again and it was going to be horrendous. But, of course, it wasn't and most of my friends are still around. (George)

Whilst Stephen commented:

I was very lucky in that I started to work in theatre and that helped me a lot. Because when you don't know gay people you have a stereotype of them and it's not till you start to work with them or meet them socially that you realise they are like everybody else. Somebody who influenced me was Steven Carrington in Dynasty, that was the first out gay that I'd seen on television, there was nobody else, there were other characters on Brookside or Eastenders but I didn't agree with that, I felt they were showing us in a negative way. (Stephen)

Some others decided to look for other gay people either through magazines' contacts or by visiting gay venues. For example:

My first experience was a black guy from Ghana. He sort of brought it out of me a bit. He was gay himself, and he introduced me to a gay club there. But that was up there in Manchester. So, when I came down to London, I thought to myself, I'd better go outside and meet some people. I went to a class where they talked about gay literature and so I met some people there. It started with a Chinese guy. So I started going out to clubs with him, all around here, and that's how I came on the scene. (Kadir)

For Lou, his first visit to a gay bar marked the beginning of a new chapter in his life:

She took me to a gay bar in London which I thought was the strangest place on earth because it was the first time for me going into a gay place. Everybody was looking at me because I was new in there, it was nice because then I discovered that there was gay places and straight places where gay people go and socialise and I liked it. After that I was going only to gay places. (Lou)

Similarly, for Nick:

Like I remember going to Heaven at seventeen and it being, you know, a huge thing to me. I mean, I remember thinking, 'Oh, my God, there are men dancing', it was big relief and a happy feeling at the same time. (Nick)

Michael decided to look for other gay people through social gay groups and organisations. He said:

No, I didn't label myself after the experience. I didn't feel I had to sleep with a man in order to prove I was gay. I never felt that. I think just before my 18th birthday I used to look at magazines and see pictures and it was then that I looked at *Time Out* and I was looking at gay groups I thought that could be me. I went to a group, that is how I started. (Michael)

Commitment 'Commitment' is characterised by an increased participation in the gay community, by the development of positive gay and friendships, and by the development of a sense of validation of their sexual identity. A common way to mark the onset of this stage is for the individual to enter a 'same-sex love relationship' (Coleman, 1982; Troiden, 1979). Additionally, the emotional state embodied in this stage will be manifested in the 'coming out' process – a unique psychological phenomenon of gays and lesbians during which they disclose their gay identity to non-gay audiences (Cass, 1979). However, this is only an indication and by no means renders one's identity as homosexual. One difficulty is that not all homosexually inclined people have reached or desire to reach the stage of 'commitment'. There are some people who identify as gay and participate in the gay community but do not experience or wish for homosexual activity. And there are homosexually active people who do not identify as gay (Humphreys, 1970).

Tasos believes that once you come out to your friends and workmates the pressure is lifted and one can get on with life. He stated:

After that it became very easy to be open about being gay. It was tough twenty years ago. The difficult thing is making the decision, but once things are in perspective and the decision had been made, it was easy and once I was open, initially at work, and found that people didn't give a damn, it was even easier to carry on. What I found was people at work would stand by those who were openly gay and knock the closets. The term 'that bloody queer' was always used about those people who were going around pretending they're not. There were two occasions in the last twenty two, twenty three years that anyone's ever referred to me as 'a queer' and I got on to the people involved, who probably denied it. (Tasos)

Similarly, for George:

> Nowadays if people ask me, I would say 'Yes, I am gay'. I usually tell people anyway. I tell them I'm living with a man, that's one of the first things I tell people anyway. (George)

For some others, however, it was a painful process of searching and analysing before arriving at a stage in their lives where they can show their flag if they asked to. Lou is a prime example:

> It was the result of all these years, searching. Sometimes painful, and long ... I reached the end of the road. I liked things that my friends didn't like, different kind of music that my straight friends didn't like. Then I saw that other people like me liked those kinds of things and I said OK, that's the end of the road, I reached my destination. I am at peace with myself now, I am not afraid. I am where I am. I am not afraid of telling people I am gay and if you like it fine, if you don't go to hell. All my friends like me, they accept me, my family, so I am at peace, I know where I am going and I know what I'm going to find. (Lou)

Identity Development Models: A Critique

Troiden's model although useful in understanding the identity development has its limitations. The main one is the fact that it is a 'stage theory' model, which fails to capture the very essence of identity development, namely its progressive process nature. In his model where the individual is: in infancy firstly exposed to sexuality through early experience in a process of sensitisation; secondly, suffers identity confusion in adolescence; thirdly develops an identity assumption in adulthood; and later, fourthly, forms a commitment to a specific sexuality as a way of life; is still far too simplistic, linear and limited to modern western society to explain the complexities of sexuality. There is no automatic progression through the above-described stages; each transition is dependent as much on chance as on decision; and there is no necessary acceptance of the final destiny, of an open and 'committed' identity (Weeks, 1991).

Troiden's model assumes that if the individuals concerned do not fulfil the requirements outlined for the stage of commitment (say), then they will, by definition, have failed to reach the stage of 'commitment'. Whilst such an objection would be valid, it may lead to the questioning of the value of a stage, which seeks to represent the ultimate stage of development, yet is unable to account for many equally valid variations. Despite its revisions, it is my feeling that this kind of model remains problematic. Part of the difficulty no doubt lies with the fact that it still employs the concept of a 'stage'. Stage theory has proved useful to the extent that it has helped to conceptualise and organise certain processes but its limitations are obvious: The development of identity does not take place in stages but is a progressive process. It resembles rather:

> ... a horizontal spiral, like a spring lying on its side. Progress through the stages occurs in a back-and-forth, up-and-down fashion; the stages overlap and recur in somewhat different ways for different people. (McWhirter and Mattison, 1984)

Apart from standarising development, the concept of stage also implies that the completion of each stage is necessary before the next one may be entered. In addition, the model assumption's of a single path to the assumption of a mature homosexual identity fails to accommodate alternative identity development and neglects the element of choice. As I have discussed earlier on, Troiden does not make clear why the sensitisation stage is necessary in the eventual adoption of a homosexual identity. Personally, I see no reason why for all homosexuals, there should exist a history of (gender) non-conformity, nor even an imperative to assume that any single instance of such non-conformity ever existed. It is my feeling that sensitisation as portrayed here is not a pre-requisite in the development of homosexual identity but rather an 'optional extra', an 'add on' experience that may or may not occur.

Mike's experience supports the above argument:

> It wasn't a case of knowing what was wrong, or feeling somewhat different from your peers. You cannot explain it at that age, you don't know what sexuality is, so all we both knew (his cousin and himself) was that we felt close to each other ... It wasn't that we were doing anything bad, nothing like that. To me it seemed natural ... the feeling of intimacy with another man. (Mike)

Similarly, Oz didn't report feeling 'very much' or 'somewhat' different from other boys:

> ... At kindergarden I remember a couple of boys I used to mess around with, and in particular one little boy used to show me his willy and I used to look and feel fascinated but I was too nervous to do anything. I didn't feel I was doing anything wrong or bad. On the contrary I thought all the boys were engaging into that type of games. I didn't see it as anything that wasn't normal. It was much later when I grew up through my family's comments, the television and the media that I knew that I was different but I didn't think there was anything wrong with it. (Oz)

Equally, Nick's childhood did not show any 'generalised feelings of marginality'. He said:

> Well, I can remember being in our second house, which means that I must have been more than eight, and I remember that I was much more interested in taking my clothes off with little boys than with little girls. I mean that's a vivid memory. And I have a memory about, maybe having sex, when I was six or something, if you can call it sex with a boy, who was my best friend, called Richard. So, whether I was aware of difference, I don't think I was aware of difference until much later in my life. I think up until then I thought that's what everybody does. No, I didn't feel that I was an outsider as we all used to mess around. (Nick)

As a conclusion, I would suggest a rather different approach to the concept of identity development as proposed by Troiden: a model based on a *processual cycle* as opposed to a periodised or stepped model of linear development. This cycle consists of four phases, in application to homosexuality, namely 'feeling different', 'coming out', 'gaining experience' and 'settling down' or 'forming relationships'.

The point is, though, that this process never stops, never reaches an end point, is never complete, and most importantly repeats as identity is never static. For example, perceptions of sexuality are constantly in process and this potentially impacts upon practices of sexuality; or, alternatively, practices of sexuality may impact upon perceptions of sexuality which are, in turn, at least partly related to coping with or consolidating sexuality.

The Management of Stigma

As we have seen above, an individual might have formed a positive sexual identity and disclosed it to a number of life spheres but still refusing to 'come out' in all social situations. Coming out to family, friends, employer, and the community involves different social interactions with each one involving a reoccurrence of the different stages and the conflicts they represent. Furthermore, the 'coming out' process does not make things simpler for the management of stigma. Originally, stigma was referred to the markings the Greeks gave to those whose social status they wanted to exhibit:

> The signs were cut or burn into the body and advertised that the bearer was a slave, a criminal, or a traitor – a blemished person, ritually polluted, to be avoided, especially in public places. (Goffman, 1963, p.11)

Nowadays, the term is more usually employed as a sociological metaphor but nevertheless is can still refer to outward signs of imperfection or irregularity (such as disability). Goffman (1963) proposes three different types of stigma: Firstly, we have the 'abominations of the body' as described above; secondly, there are 'blemishes of individual character' amongst the extensive register of which he includes homosexuality, and finally, there are the stigmata of race and religion capable of 'transgenerational communication'. What is left represents the 'normal' part of the population. Stigmatisation gives rise to the following two problems:

- The way those who are stigmatised are subject to constraints regarding the way in which they understand themselves.
- Prejudice and discrimination accompanies the stigmatised persons.

In the following paragraphs I will examine the first point in greater detail:

The concept of ambivalence As Goffman (1963) points out, the stigmatised persons tends to minimise the validity and reality of the discrimination they experience as a result of their differences and believe they are treated the same. More specifically, he argues that:

> ... a stigmatised person is first of all like anyone else, trained first of all in others' views of persons like himself (p.160) ... the standards he [sic] has incorporated from the wider society equip him to be intimately alive to what others see as his failing, inevitably causing him, if only for moments to agree that he does indeed fall short of what he really ought to be. Shame becomes a central possibility .... (p.18)

Furthermore, the individual feels that his personal lifestyle and sexual preference have limited consequences in his life and as a result he experiences feelings of anger, insecurity and frustration. The fact that he does not fit into the 'normal' section of the population has left him with an inferiority complex in the eyes of the others. Goffman goes on to note that in addition to the tendency to ambivalence, 'deviants' exhibit a tendency similar to 'normals' to stratify their compatriots in terms of the extent to which their deviance is visible. The duality of this practice lies in the fact that the deviants have the opportunity to bring to the surface the negative feelings that they naturally have towards homosexuality in the same way that 'normals' express their repulsion.

> ... the stigmatised individual may exhibit identity ambivalence when he obtains a close sight of his own kind behaving in a stereotyped way, flamboyantly or pitifully acting out the negative attribute imputed to them. The sight may repel him, since after all he supports the norms of the wider society, but his social and psychological identification with these offenders holds him to what repels him, transforming repulsion into shame .... (Goffman, 1963, p.131)

Examples of the above will be the anti-Semitic Jew, the racist black, and the homophobic homosexual who will all suffer debilitating crises of ambivalent identity since they are unable to fit into their society and yet they are not in a position to completely reject it.

When it comes to homosexuality, identity ambivalence is visible when gay men disapprove of other gay men's manners or activities, which may lead to public alienation. A good example would be the dislike that a lot of gay men have towards 'camp', 'effeminate' gay men or gay 'clones' with short hair, moustache, check shirt, ripped blue jeans and Doc Martins boots. The ironic thing, however, is that traditionally men's behaviour within the homosexual subculture has assumed the form of 'camp' – the suppression of 'masculine' behaviour for a type of parody of 'femininity'. But 'camp' was about more than men pretending to be women. It was seen as involving a positive aesthetic sensibility: a sense of beauty, and a sense of pain (Segal). 'Do you know what 'camp' is? 'high camp evangelist Christopher Isherwood (1958) asks in one of his novels, written in the early fifties:

> ... You thought it meant a swishy little boy with peroxided hair ... pretending to be Marlene Dietrich ... What I mean by camp is something much more fundamental ... You can't camp about something you don't take seriously. You're not making fun of it; you're making fun out of it. You're expressing what's basically serious to you in terms of fun and artifice and

elegance. Baroque art is largely camp about religion. The ballet is camp about love ... I admit it's terribly hard to define. (Isherwood, 1958)

Some respondents in this research were found to display greater or lesser degrees of ambivalence:

> I don't like the word queen, I don't like that. I am gay, I am proud to be gay but I like a man being a man. I am a man. A man who likes other men. I don't like feminine men. I like men. A man has to be a man, has to be tough, strong, he has to walk like a man. I don't have anything against drag queens or effeminate men, but I don't like to be seen socialising with them. I don't hate them but I never go out with them. (Lou)

The control of information disclosure Sexual stigma is different from the stigma attached to race as unlike skin colour, sexual preference is not visible. Goffman (1963) described a process individuals experience as a function of their known identity as minority. He used the concept of 'discredited' for those who were of a racial or ethnic minority group and 'discreditable' for those who required disclosure in order to be identified as a minority. For the 'discredited' the issue is managing the tension generated during social contacts (e.g. deformity), whereas for the 'discreditable' the issue is managing information about the potential tensions that could be generated if their minority status was disclosed or revealed (e.g. one's sexual preference). Following the above, the stigma carried by most non-heterosexuals is, in a sense, optional and many elect to conceal their deviance and 'pass' (Goffman, 1963) as heterosexuals. This strategy (i.e. of passing) gives the chance to the 'discreditables' to find out how others feel about the issue of homosexuality and how they would have reacted should they ('the discreditables') disclosed their sexual preferences to them. The problem in each case is:

> To display or not to display; to tell or not to tell; to let on or not to let on; to lie or not to lie; and in each case, to whom, how, when and where. (Goffman, 1963, p.129)

The following is intended to briefly identify some of the alternatives open to the homosexual who passes in all contexts and there is an attempt to either verify or exemplify these from the researcher's interviews. In total six alternatives will be examined: Counterfeit Roles; Heterosexual Courting/Marriage; 'Keeping Mum'; Disavowal; Covering; and Remoteness.

(i) Counterfeit Roles
This method allows the individual to tender the manifestations of one's real stigma as evidence of a lesser taint. Lemert (1951) refers to these guises as 'counterfeit roles'. One example would be those people with stammering problems may attempt to give the impression that they are simply 'not very talkative' or 'not very keen on large social gatherings'.

... Last Sunday, my mum asked me 'Well, aren't you ever going to get married?' I said 'Maybe after I'm forty. At the moment I want to enjoy my life'. That's the usual excuse I give her every time she asks me. (Kadir)

(ii) Heterosexual Courting/Marriage

Most 'discreditable' people are aware of the fact that if they appear to be courting a member of the opposite sex, then as far as the bulk of society is concerned, they must be heterosexual. Furthermore, some gay men go one step further and they get engaged or married in order to avoid the stigma of homosexuality. Some do it thinking that their homosexuality would simply disappear, others are fully aware of their sexuality but due to family pressures they decide to get married in order to pass (Hill,1987). For example, Georgis told me:

The point is, that I do feel very good when I go out with girls, I feel extremely good, I feel very happy and very comfortable. I enjoy being in a non-gay environment. I despise the gay scene. I really do. And if it wasn't for my friends, I wouldn't chose to go to these places. Probably I would force myself to go down to Hampstead Heath whenever I wanted a physical contact. (Georgis)

(iii) 'Keeping Mum'

By far the most popular method of passing that came up during a lot of the interviews by Cypriots who were not open about their sexuality. The reason why this is so popular lies with its passive nature. Not everybody likes confrontation and the fact that the individual has to remain silent on the issue, makes it a convenient option for the passing homosexual. Andrew, working for a Cypriot organisation said the following:

If people ask me at work I would try and change the conversation. It's a very Greek environment my work place and I don't want any problems there. (Andrew)

People at work amaze me with what they say. A woman said the other day, it's alright what lesbians do but it's disgusting what men do. Another woman, really quite religious, I got on well with her, you wouldn't think she was so anti-gay, she said once it turns my stomach what gay men do. I never came out as being gay there because, I always feel it's nobody's business and I'm on contract there so I don't want to be terminated for any reason. That's why I keep quiet and I try and do my work and then go. (Stephen)

(iv) Disavowal

Here the individual completely denies his sexual orientation. He may also, denounce of others who are open about their (homo)sexuality in order not to arouse suspicions.

John, in his twenties, said:

There was a stage when I was about 16 when I was pressured into getting off with girls. The first person I ever got off with was a girl, she looked like a man! I went out with a girl for a week but I knew it was all wrong and I finished it very quickly. I didn't want to lead her on. I didn't tell her why, maybe if I did it would have helped because she really liked me. (John)

Mike also stated:

Well up until a few years ago, I thought maybe I'm bisexual and I always thought of myself, maybe I am, yes, bisexual. I tried to have a relationship with a girl to convince myself and then convince everybody else around me. (Mike)

(v) Covering
This strategy is distinct from passing and it combines techniques of the stigma management and information control. It is Goffman's belief that 'Many of those who rarely try to pass, routinely try to cover' (p.126). By covering, the individual tries to protect the harmony of the social intercourse by 'playing down' the knowledge of others about his or her stigma. In a way there are some similarities between passing and covering, as in the instance of the homosexual Cypriot who takes a female friend at home or 'deliberately making homophobic remarks' when in the company of other male Cypriots. However, in passing the individual attempts to disguise his sexual orientation whereas in covering, the 'stigma' is camouflaged in such a way as to allow the 'normals' to deal with it in the most regular and 'civilised' way. It is my feeling when it comes to the issue of homosexuality, that 'covering' is in fact a decorative term for 'respecting others' views and 'not ramming it down their throats'.

In the case of Fotis:

If my parents or any members of my family make any homophobic remark I try and keep quiet or sometimes I may join in just to give them the impression that I agree with what's been said. I hate doing this but that's the only way to keep them from suspecting. (Fotis)

Georgis sometimes asks a female friend to phone at home and ask for him so that his Mum would stop nagging him about girlfriends. He commented:

Often, I would ask a girlfriend to phone at home and ask for me so that my mum can see that I mix with girls and therefore she would not suspect anything. (Georgis)

(vi) Remoteness
This method is more concerned with the management of social networks than with face-to-face encounters. Here the 'discreditable' individual starts distancing himself from those 'normals' that represent a real threat upon discovering his sexual preferences. The concept of remoteness can be further subdivided into the following two groups:
Yannis said:

Once I accepted my sexuality and started going out, I deliberately avoided places where I would bump into people I knew and also I tried to divide my friends into people who knew and people who didn't. It was a real effort as at times I caught myself feeling tired of all the lies and constant planning. (Yannis)

(a) Compartition

Davies (1983) challenges a central assumption of traditional accounts of coming out in which sexual identity will become the primary identity. Indeed, he suggests that there will be cases in which this is an impossible or highly unsatisfactory possibility. He then proceeds to suggest ways in which the resulting strains are accommodated and managed. He identifies two sub-divisions of the 'remoteness' technique. Compartition provides the 'structural safety' to the individual to divide his social circle (usually, family, straight friends, gay friends, work colleagues) into discrete groups maximally separated from each other in order to avoid information passing from one to another. Usually, the longest the geographical distance between the various groups the better chances the individual has in protecting his 'discreditable' identity. Goffman (1968) comments:

> Just as the individual's world is divided up spatially by his social identity so also is divided up by his personal identity. There are places where he is known personally [and] secondly there are places where he can expect with some confidence not to 'bump into' anyone who knows him personally and where he can expect to remain anonymous. (p.104)

An ideal scenario would have been the members of respective groups to be unknown to each other as acquaintance overlaps represent an obvious and dangerous source of leakage. What represents a possible threat to this method is that of 'friends of friends' link. It is impossible to know in every instance one's associates' movements especially of the more distant ranges of the network.

It is worth mentioning that the method of compartition has little appeal to those who are in no sense gay identified, who are married, who have no gay friends, or for whom the only homosexual outlet may be anonymous sex, often in 'public' places. In such instances, there are no groups that need to be segregated as the individual does not come into contact with any concrete homosexual groups nor does he desire to apart for his search for sexual liaisons, which requires little social active organisation. The only problem with that is when those people are seen by others or apprehension by the police. What the person who engages in covert deviant sexual behaviour fears most is discovery, exposure that might do irreparable harm to the whole network of social and psychological images we call the self. Discovery prejudices not only the current social situation, but established relationships as well; not only the current image others present have of him, but also the one they will have in the future; not only appearances, but also reputation. The stigma and the effort to conceal it or remedy it become 'fixed' as part of personal identity (Goffman, 1963). Davies, however, suggests that Compartition often is a short-term solution that leads to 'collusion' once the first cracks in the above discussed approach become apparent.

Costas, spoke of the difficulties that he had to face:

(b) Collusion

> I used to avoid going to places that other Greek people might hang out. Sometimes I would meet another Greek gay man in a club or bar and I would pretend that I was Italian or Spanish. I didn't want anything to do with the Greek community and especially with Cypriot gay men. I suppose it was fear that once I gave them my telephone number and name they would out me to my family. (Costas)

This is a less structured tactic than the Compartition one. It is characterised by the use of groups, which consist both of people who are aware of the actor's sexual orientation (it could be other non-heterosexuals or sympathetic heterosexuals of the same or opposite sex) and those that the actor does not wish them to know. It is not always possible for the non-heterosexual actor to keep entirely separately his double identity and often he decides to disclose some information to selective audiences thus allowing him some flexibility (Bell and Weinberg, 1978; de Monteflores and Schultz, 1978). How much does one disclose and to whom are crucial questions that the 'discreditable' actor has to consider before entering the 'discredited' arena of the public domain. It is after all, a complex strategy and requires a lot of planning and cooperation between those 'in the know' and the unsuspecting. This strategy allows some form of control by the actor over those persons 'in the know'. Furthermore, as Davies (1983) argues, any 'weak links' in the system can be easily overcome by the actor coming out to the individual concerned and sworn him or her to secrecy thus expanding the 'conspiracy' group.

Yannis commented:

> I've got a girlfriend that I've known for years. She comes round to my place and spends time with my family and especially my Mum. She knows about me and she would do anything to help me. She even offered to marry me just to keep the family happy. Although this arrangement works for the moment it doesn't make me happy and sometimes I get angry with myself with all the lies. (Yannis)

Finally, the two methods (compartition and collusion) and the various techniques they each employ are not mutually exclusive and should not be seen in isolation. Each may be used in conjunction with the other; indeed, Davies reports that a mixed combination would appear to be the preferred choice in most cases.

Coming Out

Coming out, or proclaiming one's sexuality, is commonly seen as a unitary or uniform phenomenon. More importantly, it is a developmental process that operates on several levels, most particularly three: firstly, telling one's self that one is homosexual; secondly, telling others within the confines of a safe homosexually exclusive space or place; thirdly, telling the wider and usually 'straight' society of family, friends or workplace. As I have argued in the previous section of this chapter, the fact that an individual has developed a positive self-definition about his sexuality does not necessarily mean widespread 'coming out'. Similarly, entering the final stages of the gay identity development does not compel disclosure to others. Disclosure and coming out can be treated as two separate issues and before I proceed to analyse them, it is necessary to acknowledge alternative definitions of the 'coming out' term. Gagnon and Simon (1967) define coming out as: 'the point in time when there is self-recognition as a homosexual, and the first major exploration of the homosexual community' (reported in Plummer, 1975, p.147).

Coming out in the family How is it to come out in the Cypriot community and what are the consequences of one's decision to come out to his family and his friends? Fear of rejection and instant withdrawal of family love and support forces a lot of Cypriot gay men to remain in the closet, to restrict disclosure and build a self-defence mechanism of passing techniques. The preceding analysis illustrates that passing techniques are widely adopted. However, there is a number (small though) of Cypriot gay men who have decided to come out despite the various strategies available to them. In the course of my research I have encountered Cypriot gay men with a variety of experiences with their parents. Many are afraid to disclose and may never do so. Some, who have come out, are met with hostility and rejection. A smaller number have come out and surprisingly the parents have reached a personal understanding of their son's sexual orientation that, distorted or not, enables them to come to terms with it. Those who have decided to come out do so for several reasons. The two most common reasons that emerge from the research sample are: the constant fear of being found out means that coming out is more of a pre-emptive strike than an act of self-affirmation; coming out is a means of reducing the stress and tension caused by them living a 'double life' based on fear, deception and lying.

What characterises the 'coming out' process is the transformation of the passer's situation from a 'discreditable' to a 'discredited' one. Also, it substitutes the passing strategies with management or 'coping' strategies. I would suggest that this change, although important, does not come as a surprise to the passer who during his 'probation' period has managed to equip himself with the strength and maturity necessary for their first public disclosure. The process of coming out is not an ineluctable one of psychological necessity, but one that is situated in and influenced by a real and immediate social context. Its success is normally contingent upon many years of delicate negotiation and is initiated only towards the end of the personal acceptance process (e.g. Dank, 1971; Cass, 1979, 1984; Plummer, 1975; Minton and McDonald, 1984). It is a terrifying, challenging and testing experience that is normally irrevocable. Its emancipating nature makes it to be therapeutic and self-actualising. By coming out or 'going social' (Plummer, 1975):

> The individual moves from a world characterised by secrecy, solitude, ambiguity and guilt to a subworld where homosexual-role models are available, where homosexuality may be temporarily rendered public ... A highly diffuse, unstructured experience, somewhat akin to anomie, becomes translated into one that is more clearly socially organised and ultimately stabilised. (p.148)

The following examples show the sense of relief and pride that few of my respondents felt once they have come out to their families and friends. However, the majority of them still have a problem in sharing their sexuality with their families and their individual stories and personal accounts would be extensively discussed in a later chapter.

Costas, however, stated:

> I don't think I could have done it differently. I think what I would have liked to have done differently is at the time when I told my Mum and she said to me I don't want your Dad to know, if I could do it again I would insist that she told my dad. So I knew he knew. But there wasn't any other way to do it. (Costas)

Additionally, Tasos said:

> Most of my family knows. Most of my friends know. I work with computers, but for a little while I had a building company and I did a lot of building work and fair amount of that was in Paddington at some Greek-Cypriot owned hotels, where I just gutted them and rebuilt them. My boyfriend at the time, someone who I had been with for thirteen years, was working with me and we were very open about the fact that we were gay. We didn't have any problems and we were very much liked and accepted. (Tasos)

Queer Theory

Introduction

In the early 1980s two important events were conspiring to put lesbian and gay life into crisis:

Firstly, a backlash against homosexuality, initiated by the New Right but widely supported by neo-conservatives and mainstream Republicans, punctured illusions of a coming era of tolerance and sexual pluralism (Adam, 1987; Seidman, 1992). Additionally, the AIDS epidemic energised an anti-gay backlash and put lesbians and gay men on the defensive as religious and medicalised models, which discredited homosexuality. Both the backlash and the AIDS crisis prompted a renewel of radical activism, of a politics of confrontation, coalition building, and the need for a critical theory that links gay affirmation to broad institutional change.

Secondly, internal developments within gay and lesbian subcultures also prompted a shift in gay theory and politics. Social differences within the gay and lesbian communities erupted into public conflict around the issues of race and sex. Gay men and lesbians of colour started addressing their own needs and raising their voices. They registered sharp criticisms of the mainstream gay culture for its devaluation and exclusion of their experiences, interests, values, and unique forms of life e.g., their writing, political perspectives, cultural experiences, values, customs, relationships and particular modes of oppression. The concept of a lesbian and gay identity that served as the foundation for building a community and organising politically was criticized as reflecting a white, middle-class experience (Anzaldua and Moraga, 1983; Lorde, 1984; Beam, 1986; Moraga, 1983).

As a result of this debate originated by the gay people of colour addressing the social differences in gay and lesbian lives, questions were raised about the very idea of a lesbian or gay identity as the foundations of gay culture and politics. Some members in the gay community reacted to the 'crisis' by reclaiming their power to try and unify homosexuals in the face of a political backlash, to defend themselves against the attacks prompted by the New Right, and to overcome growing internal discord.

Many activists and academics, however, started forming a new group affirming a stronger thesis of the social construction of homosexuality that took the form of a radical politics of difference. That forms the basis of the social context that gave rise to Queer theory. Although people of colour and sex rebels pressured gay culture in this direction, there appeared a new cadre of 'Queer' theorists. Influenced profoundly by French poststructuralist and Lacanian psychoanalysis, they have altered the terrain of gay theory and politics (e.g., Sedgwick, 1991; Butler, 1991; Fuss, 1991; de Lauretis, 1991; Warner, 1993; Doty, 1993).

The main argument of Queer theory is its challenge to what has been the dominant foundational concept of both homophobic and affirmative homosexual theory: the assumption of a unified homosexual identity. It is argued that Queer theory contests this foundation and therefore marks the very end of Western homosexual politics.

Queer theorists argue that identities are always multiple or at best composites with literally an infinite number of ways in which 'identity-components' (e.g., sexual orientation, race, class, nationality, gender, age, able-ness) can intersect or combine. Any specific identity construction, moreover, is arbitrary, unstable, and exclusionary. Identity constructions necessarily entail the silencing or exclusion of some experiences or forms of life. Additionally, rather than viewing the affirmation of identity as necessarily liberating, Queer theorists view them as, in part, disciplinary and defining selves and behaviours and therefore excluding a range of possible ways to frame the self, body, desires, actions, and social relations. This approach (i.e. viewing identities as multiple, unstable, and regulatory) presents Queer theorists with a series of new and productive possibilities. They argue that their aim is not to abandon identity as a category of knowledge and politics but to render it permanently open and contestable as to its meaning and political role. The gain is that it encourages the public surfacing of differences or a culture where multiple voices and interests are heard and shape gay life and politics. Queer theory wishes to challenge the regime of sexuality itself, that is, the knowledge that construct the self as sexual and that assume heterosexuality and homosexuality as categories marking the truth of sexual selves.

Queer theorists shift the focus from an exclusive preoccupation with the oppression and liberation of the homosexual subject to an analysis of the institutional practices and discourses producing sexual knowledge and the ways they organise social life, attending in particular to the way these knowledge and social practices repress differences. In this regard, Queer theory is suggesting that the study of homosexuality should not be a study of a minority – the making of the lesbian/gay/bisexual subject – but a study of those knowledge and social practices that organise 'society' as a whole by sexualizing – heterosexualising or homosexualising – bodies, desires, acts, identities, social relations, knowledge, culture, and social institutions. Queer theory aspires to transform homosexual theory into a general social theory or one standpoint from which to analyse social dynamics.

Queer Theory and Identity

The question of identity has been and remains at the centre of modern Western homosexual studies and politics. Analysing the historical formation of identities, their social construction or acquisition, and processes of coming out is pivotal to the sociology of homosexual desire. However, under the influence of Queer theory, recent sociological work has begun to change its approach to identity. Instead of viewing identity as something an individual learns or accomplishes or fashions as a positive basis for self-evaluation and politics, new sociological queer perspectives emphasize the unstable, multiple character of identities, the performative aspects of identity, and identity as a mode of social control.

A key assumption of the sociology of homosexuality and gay politics has been the notion that there is a common or more or less identical experience of being homosexual. For example, some sociologists argue that because all homosexuals experience the 'closet' and 'coming out', they share certain core experiences that form the basis of their identity. This notion of a common sexual identity has been understood as the basis for community building and politics. The new queer sociology has challenged this core assumption.

One could argue that an Anglo-Cypriot ethnic identity shapes homosexual experiences in ways not shaped by white Europeans. Racial or ethnic difference does not amount to merely an additional dimension of gay experience or a minor variation of a common homoerotic experience but produces a homosexual desire that is unique in certain important ways. For example, homosexuality is often viewed in Anglo-Cypriot cultures as a 'white European' experience and therefore the very idea of a gay Anglo-Cypriot identity would be viewed as contradictory. I would argue that homosexual identity never exists apart from differences of race, class, gender, age, or religion. Sexual identity should be analysed in relation to these various social differences in order to avoid suppressing the multiple ways of experiencing homosexual desire. This view of homosexual identity suggests a view of sexual and social identities as non-unitary, unstable, pluralistic, and an ongoing site of social and political conflict.

Conclusion

The paradox of this study of the development of identity is that whilst the content constantly points to the complex, contradictory, incomplete, and simply messy, process of development of identity, the presentation necessarily constantly creates the illusion of linearity and order, of a start, a middle, and an end to identity development. In addition, throughout this chapter, I tried to emphasize the importance of the processual complexity as opposed to simple linear development of identity and, in particular, sexuality and gendered identity, through an ongoing process of changes and developments.

I believe there are several conclusions that can be drawn from this study. Firstly, identity and life history are connected, though not so simply as merely an internalised construction, it is an interaction. Secondly, that sexuality is constructed, though on many far more complex and individual psychological levels than the traditional definition of social construction commonly permits. This particularly includes seeing the family and early school life as interactive constructs: sexuality does not start with adolescent or adult linguistic definitions, it tends to start earlier in childhood conception, construction, and experience. Thirdly, sexual identity means different things for different people at different times. Fourthly, findings from this research show similarities with the arguments raised by the Queer theorists: that a homosexual identity is not simply socially learned or accomplished but is re-enacted daily through innumerable actions and always exists as a field of shifting, multiple meanings and practices.

Finally, this chapter has attempted to examine three issues central to the non-heterosexual identity, namely: the development of (homo)sexual identity, the process of 'coming out', and its alternatives (passing). Together, these issues represent a component of one facet in the 'gay Anglo-Cypriot' narrative. I now pass to a consideration of the other main aspect of that narrative, that of an ethnic identity.

Chapter 3

Three Worlds in Collision

It is only natural that they insist on measuring us with the yardstick that they use for themselves forgetting that the ravages of time are not the same for all, and that the quest of our identity is just as arduous and bloody for us as it was for them. The interpretation of our reality through patterns not our own serves only to make us even more unknown, ever less free, ever more solitary. ('The Solitude of Latin America', Gabriel Garcia Marquez)

Introduction

In the previous chapter, I have examined some central elements of the two major identities pertaining to the non-heterosexual Cypriot man. In isolation either one of these two identities may, or may not, prove troublesome on its own merits. In combination however, one might reasonably predict some degree of conflict and in this chapter, the result of the collision of these two worlds together with the difficulties arising from an ethnic minority status are examined. Firstly, the theory of marginality in particular is considered and some of its applications are introduced. Secondly, the identity formation of minority persons is examined with particular reference to ethnic minorities and ethnic minority gay men. The non-heterosexual Cypriots' 'triple lives' that may result from such marginality are explored using extracts of transcripts from the current research. Finally, the notion of divided loyalties is introduced.

Marginality

Introduction

Between the early decades of this century and the mid-1970s, homoerotic desire was defined by scientific-medical knowledge as indicative of a distinctive sexual and personal identity: the homosexual. In other words, individuals for whom homosexual desire was important in their emotional and sexual desires now saw themselves as a unique type of person. Ironically, the framing of homosexuality as a social identity contributed to the rise of homosexual subcultures. Briefly, homosexual subcultures evolved from the largely informal networks of pre-World War II, to the marginal, clandestine homophile organisations of the fifties, to the public cultures and movements of affirmation and public contestation of lesbian feminism and gay liberation in the seventies (Adam, 1987; D'Emilio, 1983; Faderman, 1981).

Integral to the redefinition of homosexual desire into a homosexual/lesbian and gay identity were the changing meanings of homosexuality in scientific-medical discourses. From the early 1900s through the 1950s, a psychiatric discourse that figured the homosexual as a perverse, abnormal human type dominated public discussion. Kinsey (1948, 1953) challenged this psychiatric model by viewing sexuality as a continuum. Instead of assuming that individuals are either exclusively heterosexual or homosexual, Kinsey proposed that human sexuality is ambiguous with respect to sexual orientation; most individuals were said to experience both hetero – and homosexual feelings and behaviour. Kinsey's critique of the psychiatric model was met with a hardline defense of the medical model (e.g., Bergler, 1956; Bieber, 1962; Socarides, 1968). At the same time, new social models of homosexuality appeared which suggested an alternative to both the biological and psychological models of psychiatry and Kinsey.

These social approaches viewed the homosexual as an oppressed minority, a victim of unwarranted social prejudice and discrimination (e.g., Cory, 1951; Hoffman, 1968; Hooker, 1965; Martin and Lyon, 1972). By the early seventies, the women's and gay liberation movements fashioned sophisticated social understandings of homosexuality. These movements proposed images of homosexual desire and identity as normal and natural; moreover, they cruised the institutions of heterosexuality, marriage and the family, and conventional gender roles for not only oppressing homosexuals but for oppressing women (e.g., Altman, 1971; Atkinson, 1974; Bunch, 1975; Rich, 1976).

The growing national public awareness of homosexuality and the rise of new social concepts of homosexuality prompted sociologists to study homosexuality. Through the early 1970s, sociologists viewed homosexuality as a social stigma to be managed; they analysed the ways homosexuals adapted to a hostile society. Sociologists studied the homosexual (mostly the male homosexual) as part of a deviant sexual underworld of hustlers, prostitutes, prisons, crusing places, baths, and bars (e.g., Reiss, 1967; Humphreys, 1970; Weinberg and Williams, 1975; Kirkham, 1971). Much of this sociology aimed to figure the homosexual as a victim of unjust discrimination. Nevertheless, sociologists contributed to the public perception of the homosexual as a strange, exotic human type in contrast to the normal, respectable heterosexual. The next section examines the homosexual man through the lenses of marginality theory and the notion of stigma.

The Concept of Marginality

Marginality is more closely linked with the concept of the 'multiple culture' than with the multiple roles and is generated by the dislocation of a person from a single culture and their affiliation to a second without the loss of the first. Robert Park, in his introduction to Stonequist's book *The Marginal Man* (1961) defines marginality as follows:

> The marginal man ... is one whom fate has condemned to live in two societies and in two, not merely different but antagonistic cultures. Thus, the individual whose mother is a Jew and whose father is a Gentile is fatally condemned to grow up under the influence of two traditions. In that case, his mind is the crucible in which two different and refractory cultures may be said to melt and, either wholly or in part, fuse. (p.xv)

Emigration is considered to be the most common cause of marginality whereby the emigrants try to learn new ways of life, customs and traditions. Previous research on ethnicity was heavily influenced by the assimilationist model. The basic ideas behind this model were born and developed by the emerging Chicago School of sociology, a body of ideas and thematic concerns taking shape in the 1910s and 1920s under Robert Park, W.I. Thomas, and others at the University of Chicago. Park developed his famous race relations cycle: the notion that immigrant groups – and, by implication at least, ethnic or racial populations more generally – typically went through a series of phases as they gradually melted into the larger society. These phases were contact, competition and conflict, accommodation, and ultimately assimilation. In this final phase, group members 'acquire the memories, sentiments, and attitudes of other persons or groups [in the society], and, by sharing their experience and history, are incorporated with them in a common cultural life' (Park and Burgess, 1921, p.735).

The assimilated person 'can participate, without encountering prejudice, in the common life, economic and political' (Park, 1930, p.281). The assimilationist model of ethnicity, was thus heavily influenced by Park and his colleagues. However, the above-described model of ethnicity (The Assimilationist Model) became increasingly problematic by the middle of the century. A series of events made the limits of assimilationism painfully clear. The following section discusses the reasons behind the collapse of the Assimilationism model and offers a search for alternatives.

The Collapse of Assimilationism and the Search for Alternatives

Two major world developments contributed to the troubles faced by the Assimilationist Model: The first was the post independence experience of the so-called 'new nations', the former European colonies in Asia and Africa, newly granted their freedom in the great retreat of colonialism in the extended aftermath of World War II (Cornell and Hartman, 1998). The second development was the experience of the more industrial parts of the world. By the 1970s, even nations in the world's most developed regions appeared to be refragmenting and 'retribalising' as ethnic and racial identities reasserted themselves. Intergroup conflicts erupted within populations who ostensibly shared elaborate and long-established civic ties.

As Cornell and Hartman argue:

> ... the problem has been not so much escaping the assimilationist model – the last major work situated explicitly within the assimilationist tradition was Milton Gordon's *Assimilation in American Life* (1964) – as reaching consensus on what should follow it. The widening gap between assimilationist theory and ethnic reality produced two seemingly contradictory scholarly responses. One, which came to be known as primordialism, suggested that the fundamental, intractable power of ethnicity had derailed the assimilation train. The other response, which came to be known as circumstantialism or instrumentalism, claimed the opposite: that ethnicity's malleability and flexibility were to blame, the fact that it was so easily affected by changes in circumstances and could be used for so many purposes. The first said ethnicity survives because it is fixed, basic to human life, 'given' by the facts of birth. The second said it survives because it is fluid, superficial, and changeable, a product of the circumstances of the moment and therefore useful. One said it survives because it is in the blood; the other, because it is in the circumstances or the interests. (Cornell and Hartman, 1998, p.48)

Irrespective of the framework employed in the study of ethnicity, however, the researcher must question whether or not assimilation has taken place within an ethnic group, and evaluate whether ethnic identification conforms to assimilation (Parenti, 1967). Empirical work will facilitate this type of evaluation. However, marginal dualism need not in itself prove problematic, and the marginal personality will be more or less acute depending on the salience of the factor, which is causing marginality (Stonequist, 1961).

The Life-Cycle of the 'Marginal Man'

Stonequist in his book describes a general pattern of development for the marginal person although he recognises that a host of factors such as their personalities, class, education and religion might affect the way that marginals individually deal with their dualism. He then proceeds to postulate three different phases of development. In the initial phase, the individual is not aware that 'the conflict embraces their own life careers'. They may acknowledge their 'marginality' but are not aware that this difference causes others to judge them as inferior. During this 'pre-marginal' phase the marginals tend to minimise the validity and reality of the discrimination they experience from the dominant culture. This initial phase is important for the future development of a marginal identity and the greater the success of the dominant culture in acquiring the loyalty of the impending marginal, the greater will be the confusion and feeling of 'not belonging' during the period of marginal consciousness. Kenan best described this pre-marginal phase in the current study.

> I knew I was sexually different when I was about six or seven. When this school inspector came round to our school, I thought he was absolutely gorgeous, very tall and dark and handsome and that's when I knew that I liked men. Therefore I've always known that I liked men. However, it was till much later that I have attached the word gay to what I was feeling. I must have been 15 or 16. (Kenan)

In the second phase the individual experiences the above described conflict and also realises that his social status carries a stigma. His marginality is observed for the first time and a period of confusion may follow during which the marginal experiences feelings of low self-esteem as his identity and social role are challenged:

> For the individual's self is an integral part of his social role and when this social role is fundamentally changed the individual's self is forced through a similar transformation. (Stonequist, 1961, p.6)

Mike illustrates this phase in the research sample:

> For years I have denied that I was attracted to men. I tried to persuade myself that I was bisexual and tried to have relationships with girls. The longest one ran for two years. I was seeing her for two years and I don't know why I did it. After, I just sort of decided this is not for me, you know, I was living a lie. She was the sort of person, you know, you know people whether they can handle it or not, and it was a person, that no, she wouldn't be able to handle it. So I split up with her giving her the excuse that I was not ready yet for a committed relationship. (Mike)

The final phase is characterised by an adjustment to the situation where eventually, self-esteem may be partially or completely reconstructed. As result of this transition (from the 'discreditable' to the 'discredited') the individual losses his marginality and becomes free to enjoy his newly acquired identity.

George said:

> It was when I was on my Theatre Design course that I decided that enough was enough and that I was never going to feel less guilty about it. I would just have to do it and just get on with it, become a real person again, you know. I was fed up with sitting at home and being alone and lonely and pretending. Once I've made that decision I became a different person. It was such a huge relief. (George)

Personality Traits

The greater the inner conflict within the individual the bigger the 'obsession' becomes with his marginality. As a result of that the whole personality of the marginal may become oriented around the conflict. This inner turmoil is explained by Stonequist through the concept of 'personality types'. As he clearly argues, the individuals who experience extreme marginality feelings are the ones who have spent most of their lives being assimilated (both culturally and structurally) with the dominant culture. This is a result of their psychological or physical expatriation. However, as Stonequist suggests, all marginals experience a certain degree of maladjustment:

> At minimum it consists of an inner strain and malaise, a feeling of isolation or of not quite belonging. This may be subtle and evanescent in quality coming and going with particular experiences and shifting moods. From an external point of view, the individual appears to be socially adjusted ... But his mind is not quite in harmony with the world. (Stonequist, 1961, p.201)

The above would appear to be applicable in the case of the non-heterosexually identified. As I have argued in the previous chapter, the young man who first experiences feelings of attraction towards members of his own sex is unlikely ever to have mixed with others who are of similar orientation. He is very much alone in the very early stages of his 'journey of discovery' as he struggles to come to terms with his non-heterosexuality. Unless he takes the initiative to 'come out' of his 'discreditable' domain he will remain feeling marginalised and isolated.

This scenario is slightly different from the heterosexual ethnic minority people who usually participate in a score of ethnic sociocultural and religious functions, adhere to religious practices, enjoy the company of fellow co patriots and exchange visits with friends and relatives. All these indicators contribute towards the development of a pride of one's heritage and culture. Where does all this leave the non-heterosexual ethnic minority man?

The marginal non-heterosexual individuals struggle to reconcile the heterosexual values they have adopted from their own culture and the dominant society with their own feelings and beliefs of what is 'ideal' and 'normal'. Realising that their orientation once made public is likely to lead to rejection they may find themselves in a state of severe confusion and crisis. They feel helpless and frustrated. Suddenly, the marginal begins to realise that:

> ... his place in the world in a way, which he had not anticipated. It delimits his present and future in terms of his career, his ideals and aspirations, and his inmost conception of himself. And it is a shock because his previous contacts have led him to identify himself with the cultural world, which now refuses to accept him. (Stonequist, 1961, p.144)

In this way any individuals who do not fit the 'heterosexual' role model will find themselves in a kind of 'no-man's' land. The fear of stigmatisation and other negative social reactions magnify their confusion. At the same time, however, they experience a regret over the loss of benefits that accompany a heterosexual lifestyle (i.e. the experience of having a family). They belong nowhere as both worlds constitute at the same time a refuge and a prison; places that are longed for in one instant and yet despised in the next. Furthermore, the constant undermining of the marginal's sexuality by the dominant society may also lead the individual to have a very low self-esteem about himself and end up loathing himself in the same way that he believes society loathes him (Adam, 1978). Equally the marginal may re-direct his hatred feelings towards the dominant society seen as responsible for the process of marginalisation. In the case of the non-heterosexual, this is manifested in what is often described as homosexual 'militancy'.

However, not all personality attributes associated with the marginal are negative. The marginals (being outsiders) sometimes are in an advantageous position to notice the inconsistencies and deficiencies of the dominant society and have a tendency to view things with a critical detachment. As Stonequist says (1961, p.155): 'The gap between its moral pretensions and its actual achievements jumps to his eye'.

The following extracts from the researcher's sample illustrates clearly the above:

> I don't regret being gay. I don't think if there was some way I could change myself into being heterosexual that I would. I am quite happy being gay. I've always seen it never as a negative thing. I believe gay people are more sensitive towards people's problems and have more compassion and understanding than any other straight person. We are different from the rest of the society and often I catch myself standing back from a situation and analyse it. I am a great thinker. As a gay person I see it as my role to educate other people and help other people. (Oz)

All the above dilemmas and inner confusion that the marginal experiences in the first two phases of Stonequist's life-cycle are resolved or at least minimised when the third phase is reached. 'Adjustment/maladjustment roles differ widely and are dependent upon the situation of the marginal' (Stonequist, 1961). The following strategies are suggested by Stonequist as ways of dealing with the ambivalence that arises from the first two phases of his life cycle:

- The first strategy that Stonequist mentions is through the 'nationalist' role. Here, the marginal seeks a position of leadership within the subordinate group in order to restore his self-respect. '... he [the marginal] can organise his attitudes and aspirations. As his group advances in organisation its power increases and it gains greater dignity and esprit de corps. This is reflected in his own personality' (Stonequist, 1961, p.160).
- The role of the 'intermediary' is the second one offered by Stonequist. This is developed when the subordinate group is too weak to permit the emergence of a nationalist role. Stonequist argues that the marginal shows an understanding and tolerance of the dominant culture and his increased objectivity permits an effectiveness in conciliatory communications. This new role may help in strengthening the confidence of the marginal as the respect of both communities is gained.
- Thirdly, the marginal is completely assimilated within the dominant culture and he gives up the subordinate identity. This may be applicable to those people who migrate to another country voluntarily and hence the process of assimilation becomes more easier and without conflict. Whether this assumption holds true for a non-heterosexual orientation remains unclear.
- Finally, the marginal may consciously choose to pass. This strategy was covered in the previous chapter.

It was not my intention through my research to investigate the first two of Stonequist's strategies. However, my contact with the Cypriot Gay and Lesbian Group suggests that both the role of the 'nationalist' and the 'intermediary' may now be found within the group. It would appear to me that the issue of a 'complete' assimilation when it comes to a non-heterosexual orientation is complex and unambiguous. It is my opinion that for a non-heterosexual individual to relinquish totally his subordinate identity (if at all possible) he must either a) yet to enter the phase of marginal consciousness, or b) consciously or unconsciously reject his sexuality. This sample, however, would not cover such persons.

Findings from this work strongly suggest that the theory of marginality applies to the non-heterosexual Cypriot men living in England. However, I believe, that Stonequist's life-cycle fails to take into account the tensions and conflicts that a non-heterosexual ethnic minority marginal man faces as a result of the multiple interactions with his ethnic community, the gay community and the mainstream white community. For those homosexual and bisexual Cypriot men the decision to 'come out' is more than a decision about conflicting roles; it is about conflicting cultures; of belief systems and value structures that are both contradictory and discrepant. The details of this 'triple' status are now examined.

Identity Formation of Minority Persons

Coming to terms with one's identity as an ethnic and racial minority gay man involves a process of awareness of this multiple minority status (Morales, 1990). During this evolution the individual tries to reconcile different dynamics that emerge from his ethnic and racial minority in contrast to the emergence of his sexual minority status. Cory and LeRoy (1963) were among the first ones to research the conflicts and struggles that ethnic minority gay men and lesbians were experiencing. Their study was based on the lives of gay Puerto Ricans and gay Blacks as being compounded by a rock-bottom social status. The concept of double stigma was first introduced and the personal accounts of those people were viewed from that perspective.

Hendin's study (1969) of twelve Black male suicides in Harlem confirmed the earlier findings by Cory and LeRoy that the double-stigma can have enormous and destructive consequences on one's mental and physical health. In their study they noted that out of the twelve suicides four related to gay men in reaction to the double-stigma of a racial and sexual minority. Furthermore, he reported that the Black men's attempt to form sexual relationships with white men resulted to an unsatisfactory form of escape from feelings of personal inferiority and rejection.

A similar survey by Espin (1987) of Cuban lesbians showed that given a forced choice eleven out of the fourteen respondents preferred to be among white lesbians than heterosexual Cubans. They have given three main reasons for their preference: Firstly, the sexual identity and emotional romantic fulfilment were among the first priorities of the respondents; secondly, the fact that they did not have any choice when it comes to their identity as Cuban; thirdly, remaining in the closet was more stressful than being openly honest about their sexuality.

Several theoretical models have been proposed for conceptualising the identity formation and development. The identity formation for lesbians and gays was extensively examined in chapter two. I would like in the following paragraphs to summarise two other models which deal with minority groups: (1) for ethnic minorities (Atkinson, Morton and Sue, 1979); and (2) ethnic minority lesbians and gays (Morales, 1983). These models have been useful in gaining a better understanding of the identity formation process for these groups.

Ethnic Minorities

> The time I missed the Greek connection was recently, last year, when I went to a Jewish Bar Mitzvah. I went away feeling extremely sad. I often get this sense of deep sadness, because there isn't a community I belong to. There's the gay community, but that doesn't fulfil me. It's not even a need, it's a sense, and yes it's a sense of belonging. When I hear Greek music being played sometimes it triggers off a sense of loss or a sense of not belonging. I felt it most strongly when I went to this Jewish gathering. (Tasos)

Having assisted the individual to become aware of the notion of multiple identities and his ability to choose, the process of change toward a positive and integrated identity begins.

Atkinson, Morton and Sue (1979) developed a model of identity development for ethnic minorities that describes a process of identity formation through developmental stages. This model is now briefly considered:

Stage 1: Conformity
This is characterised by a preference for dominant cultural values over one's own culture. The individual not only regards the dominant culture as a superior one over his own but he also has developed a set of negative beliefs that surround his own culture. The result is a mixture of self-hatred and low self-esteem feelings. There is a tendency for looking down on his community's set of values and beliefs and a mockery out of the ways his family struggles to survive within the dominant culture.

Thus George says:

> The main reason I came in England was to get away from that terrible Cypriot environment, where I could never find or that would not allow me to do anything that I really felt like doing. I prefer it here as I've got freedom of expression. There was a time earlier on when I was pretending not to be Cypriot. I hated anything that had to do with Cyprus. I was trying hard to be British in order to become part of this society, because as you know this society is so difficult to become part of. I knew the British would never come to me so I had to go to them. (George)

John's comments were even stronger:

> The attitudes to gay people in our community put you off the idea of trying to fit in because you know that if all the cards were on the table you would be treated totally differently. I think it's a case of trying to denounce anything remotely Greek. All my friends used to go to Greek dancing and things like that and I just don't want to do that. I've always tried to steer away, I don't have any Greek friends. Well, I had one but that was a long time ago. As a matter of fact I do, I've got one Greek friend and that's it. But I don't actively go out and look for people that aren't Greek. It just so happens that heterosexual Greek young people have a very different view from me about life and what's important. I remember I had a chat with some people, it was somebody's birthday and there were a couple of Greek people there and they were going on about being proud that you are Greek, which I don't agree. If you start saying things like that I think it's almost like saying I'm proud I'm Greek because Greeks are better than anybody else. The mildest form of racism in a way. I don't agree with that at all. (John)

Stage 2: Dissonance

This stage is characterised by a cultural confusion and conflict over accepted values and beliefs held by the dominant society and by their ethnic society. The individual starts challenging the dominant culture's values and beliefs as he struggles to resolve the conflicts and confusions.

> You see at that point I wanted to get away from my culture, my identity. I mean I spent years pretending I wasn't Cypriot, not that I told anyone that I wasn't. I spent my time denying it because I wanted to get away from that identity, away from what it meant for someone who is gay. Also I wanted to assimilate myself in the British society. However, as I grew older I realised that my culture matters to me and once you start meeting more Cypriots and gay men you kind of just see it as normal. (Costas)

Stage 3: Resistance and Immersion

Here the individual actively rejects the dominant society and culture and endorses only minority-held views. The values and beliefs of his ethnic culture are embraced and an increased participation in the ethnic communities' activities is noticed. He starts exploring and discovering the community's history, which reinforces the sense of belonging and strengthens the identity with his ethnic group.

This need for belonging was expressed by Kostas:

> You just have to see my house to understand me. I'm very proud about my Greek culture. I like to have things that I can identify with, things that I can look at and feel secure. So, maybe it's an excuse for security that I can look at something and think I know where I come from and know who I am. I like to speak Greek a lot of the time. I like to listen to Greek music, that sort of stuff. I also cook Greek food and I like to follow the traditions and festivals. (Kostas)

Stage 4: Introspection

This stage presents the individual's questioning of the too-narrow restrictions of the previous stage and his feelings of conflict between loyalty to his own ethnic group and personal autonomy.

George expressed this clearly:

> I think the people in Cyprus are still in an incubatory period. It would help if the law were changed, obviously, but I don't know how it can be changed, because I always think it's such an unchangeable society. I find it very depressing that there isn't even a glimmer of hope. I don't know why. I think there is a pessimistic feel to it and, from my point of view, I find Cyprus has become such an Americanised society. The American way of life has become the example that Cypriots follow and I just find that unbelievable. Instead of developing our own life-style, by taking other things from other cultures we seem to have sidestepped our culture and taken on this other incredible, horrifying giant that has changed our lives so much.
>
> People think it's sophisticated to become so westernised. I just think it's sad, not sophisticated at all, because we've lost what was there, completely. So, from that point of view, I feel very pessimistic about life in general in Cyprus. Furthermore, the gay community loses itself even more, because those values that people follow from the American films and TV programmes homosexuality doesn't really exist within those images, at all. So, in a sense, it's a double thing against the gay community. I think the only thing that gay men do in Cyprus is get married and live double lives, that's what they do, the huge majority. (George)

Stage 5: Synergistic Articulation and Awareness

At this stage the individual experiences a sense of self-fulfilment with his cultural identity and accept or reject cultural values on the basis of individual merit or prior experience. The conflicts experienced in the earlier stages have been resolved and the individual develops a better sense of control and flexibility. Broader social issues and a sense of multi-culturalism develops (Morales, 1990). As Espin (1987) noted, the previous model (Homosexual Identity Development) and this one are remarkably similar in describing a process that:

> ... Must be undertaken by people who must embrace negative or stigmatised identities. This process moves gradually from a rejected and denied self-image to the embracing of an identity that is finally accepted as positive. Both models describe one or several stages of intense confusion and at least one stage of separatism from and rejection of the dominant society. The final stage for both models implies the acceptance of one's own identity, a committed attitude against oppression, and an ability to synthesize the best values of both perspectives and to communicate with members of the dominant groups. (p.39)

Nick has spoken with clarity and maturity about the positive and negative aspects of the Greek culture as he has experienced them through his eyes:

> I also have this terrible fear, and it comes from my, my childhood, that my family are going to swallow me up, because there's a thing about Greek-Cypriot families which is so suffocating. They want to know what you're doing, who you're doing it with. And when I was very young, when I was fifteen, I managed to break away, because I got involved in Theatre, which was something none of them knew about. And it was like my refuge and it's remained my refuge. I have no dependence on my relatives. I think I have a very, very negative view of my, my ethnicity, actually if I'm honest.

He went on to say how much he respects the women in the Cypriot culture:

> I'm proud of the women in my family. I despise the men. I think that's generally how it goes. In terms of when my father died, when I was twelve and my mother was a single woman with three kids to raise, none of my relatives came helping. Not one of those men who had so much money came helping my mum. And my brother and sister feel the same. So I'm proud to meet Greek-Cypriot people who have pride in themselves. I don't want anything to do with Greek-Cypriot people who are kind of like, who have got this kind of peasant mentality. I can't bear it. It's surprising how strongly I feel this, now you talk to me about it. (Nick)

Ethnic Minority Gay Men

Morales (1983) proposed an identity formation model for ethnic minority gays and lesbians that incorporates the dual minority status of this group. This process is postulated five different states. Each state is accompanied by decreasing anxiety and tension through the management of the tensions and differences. As cognitive and lifestyle changes emerge the multiple identities become integrated leading toward a greater sense of understanding of one's self and toward the development of a multi-cultural perspective. The advantage of this model is that it proposes different states rather than stages. Therefore, it is possible that persons may experience several states or parts of states at the same time, unlike a stage model in which resolution of one stage leads to another. In the following paragraphs the different states are considered:

State 1: Denial of Conflicts
During this state the person tends to minimise the validity and reality of the discrimination they experience as an ethnic person, and believe they are treated the same as others. Their sexual orientation may or may not be defined, but they feel their personal lifestyle and sexual preference have limited consequences in their life. They may identify themselves as gay or bisexual. Morales argues that an idealistic and utopian philosophy of life tends to dominate their perception of reality and their ability to predict how others see them. The problems they usually face is of limited friendships and being perceived as easily manipulated by the dominant sources of power. They tend to attract white lovers with the central focus of attraction being race or ethnicity. For example, Andrew, said:

> At first, I thought it would be really nice to meet another Cypriot. They're far and few between, and the Cypriots that I did meet, they were all queens, very camp, very very camp. And I couldn't really take that being camp. I was attracted to the English men from the start. They are different, more open, more free. (Andrew)

State 2: Bisexual Versus Gay
In this state there is a preference for some ethnic minority gays to identify themselves

as bisexual rather than gay. They sense that they feel neither exclusively heterosexual nor exclusively homosexual. Upon examining their sexual lifestyles there may be no difference between those who identify themselves as gay as compared to those identified as bisexual. Can the above cause a conflict in their sexual identity formation? Morales believes that it cannot as the ethnic minorities distinguish a difference in two ways: Firstly, in the way they conceptualise and perceive sexuality; and secondly, in the way they perceive the gay community as an extension of the white racist society. It may be the case that for some, sexuality is a sexual attraction for someone regardless of sex. Even if the person may lead an exclusively gay lifestyle he still may be perceived as having a bisexual identity. Furthermore, assuming a bisexual identity may also be used to avoid being labelled and categorised. Mike provided a good example of that:

> In the beginning I thought that I was bisexual and I tried to have various relationships with girls. Looking back it was a disaster but my strong family values and traditions stopped me from accepting my sexuality. Also I was thinking by being bisexual the blow to my mother wouldn't be that hard if suddenly my secret was discovered. (Mike)

Another way sexuality may be viewed by the ethnic minority person is by perceiving the gay community as white, as not inclusive of people of colour, and thereby as racist. The Anglo-Cypriot gay men may experience the challenges of being racial and ethnic minority persons as extraordinary both in the mainstream society and in the white gay community. As a result they prefer to socialise with the Cypriot community and to be referred to as bisexual rather than gay. However, a problem that arises is that the perception of a Cypriot gay community may not be realistic for them.

The following example supports the above argument:

> I had an English lover for a year. He said he loved me and I hoped that I would grow to love him but I didn't and that's why it ended in the end. I didn't like the way he treated me because he had a stereotype image of a Greek-Cypriot man would be and I wasn't that. Well, you know like you get a lot of English people who just like going out with black people, I suppose there is a stereotype there and I suppose he thought he was going out with a Greek-Cypriot stud and I didn't do anything to dispel the myth and I got a bit tired of it in the end. He couldn't understand my upbringing because his was different to mine, he couldn't understand my relationship with my parents, the fact that I had to spend a lot of time at home. It's different for English people, they tend to leave home when they are 16 or 17. You should enjoy being with someone and if you don't then that's it. (Stephen)

State 3: Conflicts in Allegiance
During this state the member of an ethnic minority becomes uneasy and uncomfortable as he becomes aware of both his ethnic minority status and his homosexuality. The ethnic minority person faces a series of dilemmas (e.g. mixing the different parts of his life; keeping them separate; about taking sides; about betraying either the ethnic minority or the gay community), which cause him a lot of anxiety and concern. His ethnic background dictates to him the importance of the family as a means of survival

against the mainstream society. The gay community points to the common struggles of gays as a way to emphasise the need for unity across cultures and nationalities. Morales suggests that such dilemmas provoke uneasiness as the ethnic minority gay man fluctuates among them. He then introduces the notion of multiple identities as a means of reducing the conflict. Enabling the person to prioritise these allegiances and examining the supportive aspects of each community tend to shift the conflict from a monocultural perspective into a multicultural dimension in which his life can be viewed as containing multiple identities.

Kenan said of this 'multiple identities' syndrome:

> If I told my parents it would affect my outlook and the way I look on this country. I cannot do this to my family. I see them every day. I have to pretend that I am something different to them. It's hard trying to be two or three different persons at different times. (Kenan)

Stephen also commented:

> I would like to meet somebody who can accept me as I am. Somebody who is prepared to make allowances. Both my sexuality and family matter in my life. I don't see why you should choose between the two. I think you can have both but obviously if my parents knew I was gay it would make things very difficult. It's not easy but I don't want to hurt my parents, I would rather hurt myself. (Stephen)

State 4: Establishing Priorities in Allegiance

A primary identification to the ethnic community prevails in this state and feelings of resentment concerning the lack of integration among the communities becomes a central issue. There are feelings of anger and rage stemming from their experiences of rejection by the gay community because of their ethnicity. These feelings coupled with the personal history of the persons encourage a primary identification with their ethnic minority community. It is not uncommon during this state to see the ethnic minority gay man separating white gay friends from ethnic friends and developing relationships with persons who have similar community allegiances. Morales argues that the person has to be encouraged to develop a proactive rather than a reactive or victim perspective in their relationships and allegiances. An example, he continues, of a proactive, affirmative attitude is the reluctance of the individual to be referred to as an ethnic minority. The term minority carries an oppressive connotation and people should be encouraged to use their ethnic identification (i.e. Cypriot man).

Mike commented:

> With me, I tend to go for black guys. I've got more in common with the Black people than with Greek people. I haven't gone out with a Greek guy. As a matter of fact I haven't gone with too many white guys because they don't turn me on as much and they don't have the same common knowledge as, you know, a black guy would. I feel the black people are discriminated by the British society like gay men are by the straight people. (Mike)

In addition, Kenan, said:

> I always thought that gay men were strong but I saw that as being a complete lie. One thing it made me very anti white men. David only ever went out with Asian and black men. I was the lightest man he ever went out with. A colonial fantasy definitely. But a colonial fantasy in reverse because he wanted to dominate because even with sex he saw sex as power. (Kenan)

State 5: Integrating the Various Communities
As a gay person of colour the need to integrate his lifestyle and develop a multi-cultural perspective becomes a major concern. Optimising the use of social and support groups becomes more important. Adjusting to the reality of limited options becomes a source of anxiety, facilitating feelings of isolation and alienation. The pressure to be the bridge between their ethnic minority community and for the gay community presents a constant challenge to the issues of allegiance and may result in feeling misunderstood. According to Morales the anxiety and tension around these issues can be minimised if the ethnic minority gay man is encouraged to build his confidence in his judgment in assessing others and expanding his support system to include persons with similar multicultural perspectives.

The advantage of this model, is that it proposes states rather than stages suggesting that individuals may find themselves at one or more states rather than at a particular stage. For example a person may identify with being bisexual yet live an exclusively gay lifestyle (State 2), and have a strong identity to his ethnic minority community (State 4). The models of Atkinson, Morton and Sue, and of Troiden, can be integrated and applied using these states. Hence, this multi-state individual can be in Stage 1 of Troiden's model and Stage 3 of Atkinson, Morton and Sue's model. Such a person may experience much anxiety about others knowing his sexual preference, decide to identify as a bisexual in reaction to the lack of support they feel in the gay community due to discrimination and prejudice, and reject the dominant society's beliefs and values because of its history of oppressing minorities.

Ethnic Minority Gay Men: Psychosocial Factors

The life of a British-born Cypriot often means a life that is lived within three communities: the gay community, the Cypriot community, and the predominantly white heterosexual mainstream society. Each community has its set of norms, values, and beliefs, some of which are fundamentally in opposition to each other. Some choose to keep each community separate, and others vary the degree to which they integrate the communities and lifestyles. Each community offers important aspects supporting lifestyles and identities. Each community can be self-sufficient if the individual chooses to stick with a particular one. The gay community offers support in the expression of one's sexual orientation identity, the Cypriot community offers emotional and familiar bonding as well as cultural identity, and the mainstream society offers a national and international identity as well as a mainstream culture and multidimensional social system.

In an ideal world a gay person of colour would have drawn resources from and maintain associations with each of the three communities. But as Carballo-Dieguez (1989), Espin (1987), and Morales (1990) have suggested, such associations carry negative consequences with them. Their ethnic minority community has homophobic and negative attitudes toward gays in general; the gay community is a reflection of the mainstream white community and mirrors the racist attitudes toward the gay men of colour through discrimination and prejudice; the mainstream white heterosexual community embraces the homophobic and negative attitudes toward gay as well as the racist attitudes and practices toward the gay men of colour. As a result of the above the Cypriot gays find themselves weighing the options and managing the tensions and conflicts that arise as a result of the multiple interactions (de Monteflores, 1986).

Cypriots have traditional value systems (although class divisions do exist both in Cyprus and among Greek-Cypriots in Britain. These are largely due to socio-economical and political reasons), and the sex role expectations are similar to those of other cultures with the rigid assignment of sex roles leading to sexism. Homosexuality is not an exemption. Being a non-traditional lifestyle it carries all the negative attitudes and connotations that one would expect to find in any sexist society and that includes the Cypriot culture. As the Cypriot gays develop their sexual orientation, the gender role models parallel those of the socially accepted heterosexual models. Hence, individuals tend to immediate and follow certain sex roles as the heterosexuals, except that both gender roles can be found among gays rather than being sex specific. Therefore, some Cypriot gays may identify more with effeminate characteristics (e.g. drag queen) and others may identify with masculine characteristics usually referred to as butch.

I believe that the influence of socio-economic class and articulation in the Great Britain plays an important role in how Cypriot gays socialise. Carrier (1976, 1977, 1989) suggests that gay men in other countries mimic gender roles within their social networks. The rigid gender roles are carried into relationships in a similar form as in heterosexual coupling. Therefore, one can find a small number of Cypriot gays cross dressing where the individual attempts to amplify his lifestyle as well as entertaining his close social circle. The variations, however, seem to occur as a direct function of the sexual orientation identity. The more the person is gay identified the more he is prepared to accept the traditional same-sex gender roles. This seems to be a result of the negative attitudes that the Cypriot culture have towards gays combined with the traditional heterosexual expectation that children will live at home, get married, and continue the family with their own children (Carballo-Dieguez, 1989; Carrier, 1976, 1977, 1989; Espin, 1987).

Members of ethnic minority communities, as well as white gay men, often choose to view identity as if it were a singular entity. Strong attachment and identification with one's ethnic group seems to be incompatible with one's sexual identity (other than heterosexual). These two (identities) are perceived as mutually exclusive as well as other aspects of their identity.

Where does he turn for support though? A possible source is the members of the mainstream gay community who become important outlets for social and moral support during the period that his application is considered. However, gay men of colour report discriminatory treatment in gay bars, clubs, and social and political gatherings, and in individuals within the gay community (Chan, 1992; Dyne, 1980; Garnets and Kimmel, 1991; Greene, 1994; Gutierrez and Dworkin, 1992; Mays and Cochran, 1988; Morales, 1989). They describe feeling an intense sense of conflicting loyalties to two communities in both of which they are marginalised by the requirement to conceal or minimise important aspects of their identities in order to be accepted. Gay men of colour frequently experience a sense of never being part of any group completely, leaving them at a greater risk for isolation, feelings of estrangement, and increased psychological vulnerability.

Tasos spoke about the feeling of non-belonging:

> If I'm among foreigners and they ask me where I'm from I would say I'm English. If I'm amongst English people, then I'm Greek or Cypriot. I'm not English. I'm in the same boat as a lot of foreign people, not just Cypriots, it could be Indians, or any other group, who have been born over here or who have spent most of their lives over here. They identify with the English in thought patterns, but one can never belong. Yes, a lot of my thinking is influenced by my upbringing. The competitiveness is still there. The fact that I show a lot more initiative than English lads in a work environment comes from being Cypriot. I'm very glad, in many respects that my background is Cypriot because a lot of English attitudes make me cringe. I cannot stand them. The Cypriot culture is a mixture of things: I like the hospitality but you've got the nosiness on the other hand. You've got the open nature, the warmth and tactileness coupled with intrusion into your space. On top of that, you have all the homophobia that exists that makes it difficult for me to be at ease within my own culture. It's a sense of being a foreigner in your own country. That's the problem that I face sometimes in trying to reconcile my sexuality and ethnicity. It's hard you know. (Tasos)

Conclusion

Throughout this chapter I have considered the complexities of coming out in a multicultural context and attempted to highlight a number of issues that a gay ethnic man must resolve as part of the coming out process. These include: (a) deciding whether or not to disclose to the family; (b) finding a niche among gay peers; and (c) reconciling sexual orientation with other aspects of identity. For the son of the immigrants, the coming out process takes place against the backdrop of ethnic traditions, values, and social networks. For some, this adds a dimension of complexity to the issues. Homosexuality, often in conflict with Western religious and cultural mores, seems even more incongruous and unacceptable in the context of conservative and traditional Cypriot values. Furthermore, the rift that occurs between parent and child over sexual orientation is set in the context of an existing conflict as the son pulls away from the traditional Cypriot culture to espouse the Western way of life.

Two models were offered in understanding the identity development and formation first of ethnic minorities and then of ethnic minority gays and lesbians. Each model was supported with extracts from my research and experience. Most importantly, though, the men I spoke to were commonly united in their struggle for acceptance by the Greek community. Through their personal accounts the following crucial findings were emerged:

- Firstly, the nuclear and extended family plays a key role and constitutes a symbol of their ethnic roots and the focal point of their ethnic identity. The importance of a supportive family context for the survival and psychological well being of the individual has been emphasised.
- Secondly, ethnic minorities and especially the Cypriot community sometimes deny that gay men and lesbians exist within their communities and claim that homosexuality is a 'white people's problem'.
- Thirdly, for those who choose to come out in the ethnic community, reactions range from moderate acceptance to tolerance of being stigmatised and treated as an outcast. Such ostracism is extremely threatening because of the close relationship and identification with their family and ethnic community.
- Fourthly, the men I have interviewed feel deeply about their cultural roots, such that being an outcast from the ethnic community and family can result in chronic feelings of anger and isolation.

Finally, many Cypriot men that took part in this research have developed effective coping mechanisms and are successful in managing the conflicts they face. Their sexual identity is as important as their ethnic and cultural identity. I now pass to a consideration of sexuality and indeed homosexuality within the Greek culture.

Chapter 4
Cypriot Culture and Homosexuality

Introduction

In the previous two chapters, some central elements of the two major roles/identities pertaining to the non-heterosexual Cypriot man were considered. In isolation either one of these two identities may, or may not, prove unsustainable. No analysis of how Cypriot men behave and operate would be complete without some examination of the Greek-Cypriot cultural values. An appreciation is required of how Greek-Cypriot men and women perceive the world, and how they regard their role within it. In this chapter, I would like to focus on those ingredients, which culture observers have suggested contribute to the formation of a cultural and sexual identity.

Cyprus has been described by anthropologists as a society largely based on kinship. Familism is considered to be the most important orientation in Greek life. Insofar as marriage leads to the reproduction of kinship, kinship has been regarded as a fundamental principle or relatedness and a powerful idiom of action. Kinship informs the complex of 'honour and shame' values and all actions are oriented to prestige (Peristiany, 1965). It also embraces spheres of activity outside marriage; in structural-functionalist terms, it is the basis of the institutional domains of economics, politics, and religion (Loizos et al., 1991).

I will look mainly at the meanings attached to homosexual behaviour so as to show the social organisation in Greek-Cypriot society. As Gagnon and Simon (1973) argue homosexual behaviour may well be universally observed, but the meanings given to it remain culturally specific. What meaning is attached to which behaviour highlights the ways societies view sexualities. It would be wrong to say that sexuality is shaped or defined through the idea of a 'unitary society'. On the contrary, society is a regarded as a fragmented kaleidoscope made up of diverse sets of relationships, institutions, and practices that in some cases brighten or darken the lives of the individuals in it (Foucault, 1979; Weeks, 1985). Questions like 'What is homosexuality?' and 'Who is homosexual?' are open to different interpretations and answers according to the diverse cultural meanings and practices. To understand and research homosexuality in the Greek-Cypriot culture one has to examine sexuality within the society's context. The two are not mutually exclusive. The way men and women react towards issues of homosexuality have a direct relationship to the way they perceive their own feelings and sexual desires, fidelities and infidelities, sexual behaviours and sexual lives. To look only at homosexually identified people would be missing the point as the number of people who engage in homosexual behaviour is by far greater than the openly identified homosexuals in the Cypriot society. Homosexual behaviour is widely spread among Greek-Cypriot men but homosexual identity is rarely visible.

It is therefore important to raise the following issues: to ask about the cultural constructions of homosexuality versus the 'homosexual' essence; to define the various boundaries drawn around differing forms of experience; to ask under what circumstances and conditions it is permissible for the one to meet the other and to see the ways this is regulated by society; to examine how Greek-Cypriot homosexualities are linked to both sexuality and the prevalent gender system. To understand the Greek homosexuality one has to understand the polarised and fixed gender structure, which hinders the emergence of alternative models of identity for individuals. As a result of that the Greek-Cypriot homosexuals are left with nothing but clearly defined roles. It is true to say that, till recently, the majority of the homosexuals in Cyprus once they recognise their homosexuality in so doing accept their effeminacy through identifying themselves with women and the images of womanhood. As a final point the issues of family and religion as they relate to the Greek-Cypriot culture and homosexuality will be examined.

Sexuality in the Greek-Cypriot Culture

Foucault (1985) argued thus: 'One would have a difficult time finding among the Greeks ... anything resembling the notion of "sexuality" or "flesh"':

> [It is] a notion that refers to a single entity and allows diverse phenomena to be grouped together, despite the apparently loose connections between them, as if they were of the same nature, derived from the same origin, or brought the same type of casual mechanisms into play: behaviours, but also sensations, images, desires, instincts, passions. (p.95)

Although Foucault was referring to the ancient Greeks, his writing has some significance for the contemporary ones as well. Sexuality is a topic of conversation among the Greeks and often is wrapped up in layers of exoticism and mystery. Faubion (1994) remarks in *Modern Greek Lessons* that:

> 'Sexuality' in demotic is *sexoualikotita*, a blatant barbarism. Demotic offers another term, derived from the same sources: *sexoualismos*. Literally 'sexualism,' *sexoualismos* is in fact a partial synonym for the more familiar *afrodhisia*. Both *sexoualismos* and *afrodhisia* designate 'sexual instincts,' 'carnal attraction,' or 'genital arousal.' *Afrodhisia*, however, has come to have a rather special sense of its own. It is now preferred as a designation of 'venereal disease'. (p.217)

Sexual relations and acts in the Greek culture (in contrast with any traditionally personal acts and relations) are exclusively private affairs. 'Moral conceptions in Greece and Greco-Roman antiquity were much more oriented toward practices of the self and the question of *askesis* [exercise, training] than toward codifications of conduct and the strict definition of what is permitted and what is forbidden' (Foucault, 1985, p.30).

The Orthodox Church does not want to know about any sexual relations outside the marriage and when it does it condemns them; the State law remains circumspect in its dealings with them as well. Any sexual deviations from the 'norm' are severely disapproved and informally sanctioned in all social strata but the more cosmopolitan and open-minded. 'Guilt as well as shame have their effect not simply upon sexual conduct but also upon the determination of self-worth' (Faubion, 1993, p.218). The politics of the masculine and feminine comportment dictate the taxonomy upon which relations and acts whether sexual or nonsexual are being evaluated within the Greek-Cypriot culture: some acts are honourable others are not; others are shameful or degrading. This taxonomy enforces a uniform dualism: between the active and the passive; between the dominant and the submissive; between the strong and the weak. Faubion (1993) remarks that both the taxonomy and the dualism allow for their contextual variations. But both still generally govern the traditional assignation of sexually indexed roles and of sexually indexed prestige. Both still generally govern the traditional assessment of what it is, and what it is not, to prove oneself an *andras*, a 'man'.

The Honour and Shame Value System

The concept of sexual behaviour in the Greek-Cypriot culture is closely tied up with the concept of 'honour and shame' value system. This system predetermines the way Greek-Cypriot women and men view themselves in relation to issues concerning sex, moral codes and the way they are viewed by others in relation to these matters. Women are seen as passive but also as a source of danger. Their believed capacity to control their sexual urges and at the same time, the belief that men's sexual drive is natural, but uncontrollable, renders women responsible for maintaining the moral-equilibrium.

As Hirschom (1989) writes:

> Since women have the power to control their sexual urges they are at fault when transgressions occur ... The imperative nature of a man's sexual drive casts the woman as a constant potential threat. Her sexuality, if not properly controlled might undermine her own honour, that of her family, and destroy a man's integrity, seducing him away from his commitment to his own family ... Women in this view present a potential threat to the whole social order, they are powerful and dangerous. (p.149)

In reference to women's modesty Du Boulay (1974) writes:

There is still thought of as an absolute prerequisite for the honourable woman, and involves a conception of purity which places an unalterable value on the virginity of the unmarried girl and the chastity of the married woman ... honour is given to an individual by the community, and since feminine honour depends on the possession of shame, it is vital for the possessor of shame that the fact should be demonstrated to the community. It is in fact as important to be seen to be chaste as it is to be chaste. (p.111)

Over the last decade women in Cyprus started demanding equal treatment with men within the society and a lot of the younger ones have started rejecting the old traditions and values. Greek-Cypriot men, however, are still trapped within the machismo image and do not as yet have quite the same measure of liberty. They are still expected to act like *andres*, 'real men', and any diversification from that is open to questioning.

To Be or Not to Be a Man

The interviewees regularly repeated that the Greek-Cypriot *andras* 'man' is expected to be *eneryiticos*, 'energetic' or 'active' in the social sphere; he should also be *eneryiticos* as a sexual force.
As Herzfeld (1985) writes:

[the Greek man] must protect his family from sexual and verbal threats, and keep his household at a level that befits a 'master of the house [*nikokiris*]'. He must dispense hospitality at every possible opportunity, deprecating the poverty of his table while plying his guests with meat and wine. And in all these domains, his every action must proclaim itself a further proof of his manhood. An action that fails to point up its own excellence is like the proverbial tree falling in an empty forest.

Another aspect of the masculine sexuality in Cyprus is reflected in the way men are recruited into the army. The induction process into the army involves a physical inspection to ascertain that a man is not homosexual. All modern armies carry out physical inspections and whatever the military and medical rationales for these they can be interpreted (following Goffman, 1961) as one useful degradation ritual which gets the conscript off balance and suggests that the young recruit is subject to the total power of the institution, down to and including control and surveillance of his body and its functions (Loizos, 1991). Sexual preferences and orientations do matter in the army and since part of the army's mission is to turn 'boys' into 'men' those recruits that do not perform well are left open to their instructors' humiliating comments about how they resemble women. Only 'real' men are needed in the army and those who cannot exhibit the necessary macho skills are ridiculed. What survives in the memory of the candidate soldier is the physical comparison with the rest of the men who sit naked in a row, and the examination of the anus to diagnose signs of homosexuality. Despite its traumatic nature, the first day in the army, marks both a confirmation of physical masculinity and probably the first, most important, formally approved transcendence of the local boundary and a prolonged separation from 'home'.

The boy suddenly becomes a man as he passes the masculinity test and enters the military arena. However, if he fails the test then the rectum becomes his grave in which the masculine ideal is buried (Goldberg, 1994). Suddenly, the boy can no longer be a man but instead he is strongly denigrated as someone who fundamentally lacks full masculinity and his moral weakness exposes him to all sorts of evil dispositions (du Boulay, 1974; Herzfeld, 1985). Furthermore, the regulations in the Greek-Cypriot army permitted periods of leave for 'natural reasons of bodily health'. This was understood to mean heterosexual contacts which, until the last twenty years, usually involved prostitutes since young Greek males typically do no get engaged until after completing military service.[1] The modern army is no longer seeking to operate with the ideal of the virginal, continent strong man, familiar from the classic.

The Greek-Cypriot Homosexual[2]

The main categories that have dominated the Western Homosexualities studies, heterosexuality, homosexuality, bisexuality, are clearly present in the Greek-Cypriot culture. Nonetheless, they have a history that is connected as in the Western Europe and the United States, to the emergence of modern medical science. The cultural construction of homosexuality is very much interwoven with two major social institutions that seem to dominate the Greek-Cypriot society, namely the Greek-Cypriot family and the Christian religion. These two will be examined separately and in detail in the following sections.

Notion of activity and passivity The notion of a single homosexual identity or a distinct homosexual community or a gay ghetto is a notion fairly new to the Greek-Cypriot community. The structure of the sexual life in Cyprus and as result the way people perceive the concept of sexuality, has traditionally been conceived in terms of a model focused on the relationship between sexual practices and gender roles; more specifically, on the distinction between eneryitikotita (masculine activity) and pathitikotita (feminine passivity) as central to the order of the sexual universe.

In Volume II of the *History of Sexuality*, Foucault suggests that a general ethical polarity in Greek thought of self-domination coupled with a helpless indulgence of appetites has contributed towards a structuring of sexual behaviour in terms of activity and passivity, with a correlative rejection of the so-called passive role in sex (Foucault, 1985). What the Athenians find hard to accept, Foucault writes, is the authority of a leader who as an adolescent was an 'object of pleasure' for other men; there is a legal and moral incompatibility between sexual passivity and civic authority. He who reigns cannot be penetrated; he who rules cannot be dominated; the only 'honourable' sexual behaviour 'consists in being active, in dominating, in penetrating, and in thereby exercising one's authority' (Foucault, 1985).

Homosexuality in Cyprus 'originates around the schema of penetration, and in this conceptualisation the label of the homosexual is attributed to any individual who is being penetrated or thought to be penetrated, whereas the other one remains free of this label, regardless of the fact that he is engaged in homosexual sex as well' (Tapinc, 1992). The above highlights a major difference between the Western and Greek-Cypriot cultural setting for male bisexuality: the lack of stigmatisation amongst Greek-Cypriots of the active inserter participant in homosexual encounters. As a result of the above a lot of Greek-Cypriot men do not believe that 'one drop of homosexuality' makes one totally homosexual as long as the appropriate sexual role is played (Carrier, 1985). A man who takes what is termed the 'active' role, that of penetrating the *poushtis*, may sometimes be referred to by the rarely used word *kolombaras*, 'arse-taker', but he is not singled out and stigmatised.

The passive homosexual man Why is it then, that the effeminate man is judged far more harshly than the manly woman? Herzfeld (1985) argues that she may even be accorded considerable admiration and respect[3] whereas the effeminate man is a cause for ridicule. The woman who proves to be capable in both the work sphere and the good housekeeping steps beyond the traditional bounds and demands the respect of the society. She reaches for more than a mere woman would be due. However, as long as she does not neglect her feminine duties she poses no significant threat to the principles of the traditional sexual economy. Although at times she may beat the men at their own public games she does not challenge the authenticity of the games nor the prizes she tends to seek.

The dynamic, however, of the sexual economy is threatened and disturbed when a man seems to prefer the woman's world and the woman's roles. After all, he was born for the more honourable and yet chooses to settle for less; even worse: made to aspire to the more honourable, he instead rejects it for the less. The effeminate man in the Greek-Cypriot culture is among the most scorned of social subversives. He is not to be equated though with the 'homosexual'. As a result of that the visible effeminate man is considered to be more of subversive type than the man who 'is jumped', if only because he is less able to hide. The worse social stigma occurs when the visible effeminate man is also known to be a passive homosexual. He is regarded by society as the greatest subversive of all and he is widely to be not merely immoral, but mentally deficient as well.

Loizos and Papataxiarchis (1991) write in relation to the passive homosexual man (called '*poushtis*'):

> ... he is strongly denigrated as someone who fundamentally lacks full humanity, and his moral weakness exposes him to all sorts of evil dispositions ... *Poushtis* comes to be a synonym for a liar or thief, a man without dignity, and it strongly contrasts with the characterisation of the man who adopts the 'male' role and who may claim a 'supermale' reputation, much as he might if he consorted with a prostitute .... (p.227)

Male friends, especially young friends, greet or charge one another often enough with being *poushtis*, without jeopardising the friendship provided they do not mean exactly what they say. *Poushtis*, however, is not the only sexually malignant curse among friends; *malakas* (masturbator; 'wanker'), *malakismenos* (having been masturbated), and *keratas* (cuckold) are other favourite ones used in the everyday conversation. No term is more of an insult, however, than *poushtis* itself.

As Faubion argues:

> The *malakas* is least pitiable.[4] He is, if not utterly and supremely manly, nevertheless still a man. He remains a man not in spite but because of his politicoerotic solitude. If not dominating, he is at least not himself dominated. But what Brandes (1981: 227–30) asserts of the cuckold in both Andalusia and in Greece is true of *the malakismenos and the poushtis* as well: all are unmistakably feminised. Each is the patient of another's manoeuvring. Each is the victim, unwitting or willing, of a more 'energetic' and more sovereign sexual executor. The *keratas* in Greece is the victim of a stereotypical but not exclusively feminine craft: poniria, 'guile' or 'deception'. The *malakismenos* is 'manipulated'. The *poushtis* allows himself to be had. He surrenders without a fight. He unmans himself. (Faubion, 1994, p.223)

As Campell (1964) and others have remarked, the word *poushtis* in demotic Greek, signifies a man who receives another man sexually, who solicits to be penetrated, or accepts and enjoys it. The *poushtis* in the Greek-Cypriot culture, is the man who willingly gives up his sovereignty and power to control and to own. He relinquishes his masculine social being and also his claim to any social place of his own. He prefers to be identified with the passive and submissive rather than exercising his power and energy.

Social Attitudes Reconsidered

Sociologist Nikki Patsalidhou (*Omofilofilia*, 1982) remarks at a 1982 Cyprus conference on 'homosexuality' that

> old opinions ... continue even today and with the same obstinacy to present the homosexual man as the person who wants to play the role of the woman and the homosexual woman as she who identifies with the role of the man. (p.46)

She continues, however, to report on an attitudinal survey[5] taken among a group of Greek-Cypriot men willing to identify or at least to define themselves as 'homosexual'. She has found, that her respondents were semantically far more sure of themselves than the population at large:[6]

> [With] the impression that the [male] homosexual is the passive member of a sexual relation and wants to play the role of the woman, ninety-nine percent of the sample responded categorically that they did not agree ... More than half, fifty-seven percent, responded that they express themselves both passively and actively, sixteen percent only actively, and fourteen percent only passively'. (p.53)

She also reported that some 70 per cent of her respondents made every effort to 'conceal their homosexuality from those around them' (Patsalidhou, 1982, p.46). A policeman told her that were his fellow officers to learn of his habits, 'they would kill him right where he worked' (p.48). Another man told her that 'he suspected that his parents must understand, but that he could not himself accept their understanding, because he was sure that they would no longer view him as their child' (p.48). Patsalidhou also reported that some 60 per cent of her respondents conceived of their homosexuality as an 'inborn predisposition'. 'Along with it', she added, 'they nevertheless cite as contributing causes homosexual experience in childhood, twenty-one percent of them, and a dominating mother or father, twelve percent' (p.50).

Another important research (Papageorgiou, 1997)[7] that shed some light into the issue of homosexuality among Cypriot people, showed that 75 per cent of the respondents thought that homosexuality is 'always wrong' or 'mostly wrong'; 10 per cent thought that it is 'sometimes wrong' and 8 per cent believed that it's 'rarely wrong' or 'not wrong at all'. When the respondents were asked whether male homosexuality should be decriminalised in Cyprus, 41 per cent agreed with the decriminalisation and 59 per cent said that the law should stay as it is. The majority of the respondents who agreed with the abolishment of the law came from social classes 1 and 2 (managerial, professional or non-manual) had a higher educational qualifications and came from the age gap 18–44.[8]

Multiple Identities and Gay Greek-Cypriots

The Greek-Cypriot men I have interviewed accepted the fact that constructing a full gay life-style may not be feasible. The ways of coping and dealing with their sexual identity vary from person to person. However, the main aim in all the coping mechanisms is to minimise the strain on them by finding a happy medium between their sexual identity and social lives. Their personal journeys and struggles do not make them less gay than the ones who allowed their sexual identity to predominate over other aspects of their identity. It has become quite apparent from the interviews that the concept of 'multiple identities' is quite a normal thing amongst the interviewees. Sexual identity for the majority of them has not become the primary identity. A lot of them have devised various coping mechanisms and tried to incorporate their sexual identity in their everyday life. How difficult is this constant struggle to maintain that equilibrium among the multiple identities?

Mike spoke frankly about this struggle:

> The thing that I dislike is not being able to come out to my family. Once you've come out to the family and they can accept it, which I know mine won't, at least you can bring a partner home to meet the family. There's not all this secrecy, yes, and I can at least find someone who, even if he might not understand my culture, at least I'll be with them in a surrounding that I feel comfortable with. That's the only annoyance that I've got. It's not with the gay life, it's with my own cultured life, that's the difference. (Mike)

Similarly, Tasos had faced a similar situation. He spoke frankly about his personal account:

> It was a big emotional thing. It was all the guilt was piling on about my homosexuality. I convinced myself I wasn't gay. When I was about twenty-four I was at home during my Christmas holidays, and I had just about enough. I used to question the purpose of life, as one does when one is younger. I was fighting between my Greek upbringing, my religious background and my homosexuality. Well, one is going to die anyway, so I took an overdose. They reacted much quicker than I expected. My light was still on. I hadn't quite managed to get into bed to switch my light off and, unusually, my mother got up in the middle of the night and saw my light on, went into my room, which is something she rarely does. I was unconscious and I was rushed to the hospital. They kept me alive on a machine because I'd technically died, they kept me alive and forty-eight hours later, I was back to my senses. This is something I've told very few people. It's not something I'm proud of. (Tasos)

The Role of The Christian Religion

Another element that contributes to the difficulty Greek gay men face in establishing a cohesive personal identity is the position the Greek Orthodox Church takes towards issues of sexuality. Often, there is strong religious element attached to their upbringing where God represents the ultimate punishment. To fail the parents' expectations is one thing but to fail God's wishes is seen as sin. As a result of the above, Greek-Cypriot gay men internalise all these negative attitudes as gleaned from loved and trusted figures. This has a negative effect in their process of a healthy identity development and self-acceptance.

> The Greek Orthodox Religion constitutes an important feature of ethnicity for Greek-Cypriots although their orientation can be characterised as passive religiosity. The Greek-Orthodox church in Great Britain has had also a significant political role. It has a long history dating from 1676 when a colony of Greeks settled in Soho. The Aghia Sophia Church was built in Moscow Road, Bayswater in 1879. The All Saints Church was opened by Greek-Cypriots in a former Anglican Church in Camden Town in 1948. This was followed by others, outside London and in those boroughs where Greek-Cypriots live, such as Camberwell, Hendon, Wood Green, and Hackney.
>
> The Church in Britain has always been dominated by Greek priests from the mainland and has usually propagated nationalist, Rightist and chauvinist views. It set up the first Greek classes before the Second World War. (Anthias, 1992)

And what, does the Greek Orthodox Church have to say about homosexuality? A study (Georgiou, 1992 – it is believed that this is the first such study in the Orthodox world to date) examining the sexual attitudes of Greek Orthodox priests living in Cyprus on topics such as adultery, premarital sex, abortion, contraception, masturbation, homosexuality and coital abstention showed the following:

Regarding the subject of male homosexuality the following attitudes and beliefs were common to both groups:

- That male homosexual practices (it was not made clear what type of practices) were unusual, perverse and a form of disease.
- That male homosexual practices were considered to be a cardinal sin.
- That homosexual acts could be discontinued by confession.
- That male homosexual intercourse degraded man into woman. That Sodom and Gomorrah were destroyed because their inhabitants had sinned by committing homosexual acts.

The main differences between the Church Fathers and the modern day priests relate to the way homosexuals should be treated.

For example:

a) The Church Fathers recommended heinous tortures for the homosexual person, which included being hanged, drawn and quartered, or being burned at the stake. The Cypriot priests were a lot more humane. Approximately 90 per cent under the circumstances posed by the question no 6,[9] recommended termination of the sexual relationship, some priests encouraged the male couple to maintain a platonic friendship, while others advised the young homosexual to see a Christian therapist for therapy, and/or go to a Spiritual Father for confession.
b) While the Cypriot priests felt that homosexuality was a sin (40.2 per cent), the Church Fathers went further and compared it to the sin of murder.
c) The Cypriot priests tried to help by recommending that the homosexual either marry immediately (12.9 per cent), or make a confession and be cured (12.1 per cent). The Church Fathers' recommendation of ostracisation and extermination again reflect a much harsher treatment of these people, which seems incongruent with Jesus' treatment of the oppressed or the prime directive of Christianity to love one another.

It is also apparent that the pastoral advice given to the male homosexual by the Cypriot clergy is incongruous with current scientific data from behavioral and empirical studies. Also recommending heterosexual marriage to a homosexual who is only attracted to same-sex partners is perhaps not the wisest and most appropriate guidance one can give. At the very least, it ignores the expectations and feelings of prospective wives. It appears that the modern day Cypriot priests, like their predecessors, knew nothing of homosexuality: both were solely concerned with the commission of homosexual acts – an important point made by Bailey (1955). It is also apparent that the concept of the homosexual act itself is far from specific. According to McNeil (1977), there were many different names used in the Bible and by the Church Fathers for persons who practised homosexual activity.

Some of the Apostolic Fathers such as St Augustine and Lactantius expressed a profound horror at what they considered to be degradation: a man who allowed his body to be used 'as that of a woman' should 'rather die a thousand deaths than undergo this' (Boswell, 1981). Boswell believes that these anxieties about male homosexual acts are largely responses to violations of gender expectations, rather than the outgrowth of a systematic approach to sexual morality.

This attitude was also held by the modern day Cypriot priests who categorised homosexual acts into 'passive' or 'feminine', and 'active' or 'masculine', believing that there were two distinct types of homosexual persons who behaved either one way or the other. The Cypriot priests also believed that the passive homosexual was far worse than the active one, which is congruent with the Church Fathers' attitudes, and also reflects the societal attitudes of the majority of Cypriot males. It is taken for granted in Cyprus as in other Mediterranean, Latin American and Middle Eastern countries that the true homosexual is the person being penetrated. However, the active participant is not considered a homosexual, nor is he considered to be participating in a homosexual act. It is certain from anecdotal evidence that the Orthodox clergy and spiritual mentors do encounter such cases of homosexuality in their working lives, and are often placed in the difficult position of providing spiritual guidance to these people. The above results illustrate the difficulties that Greek gay men might face from the Church in trying to develop and established a happy positive image about their sexuality. The priests' comments are indeed painful as all of my interviewees still do identify as Greek Orthodox.

One of my interviewees, mentioned the following when I asked him whether his religious upbringing had any effect upon his identity and personality development.

> In fact, I felt guilty from the very onset till I was mature and understood. But the society didn't recognise what I was up to. It wasn't normal so to speak. But in addition to that, the biggest factor that induced guilt in me was the religious aspect and it run very strong in my family. While I was in Cyprus, I was quite a religious person. I used to go to the church very frequently. I used to be the priest's assistant basically. So, I saw my sexual tendencies as being in disunity with the religious teachings. So, it did bother me a lot. It still bothers me, but not as much as it used to bother me. (Andreas)

For Costas, the fact that the Church cannot embrace his homosexuality made him abstain from any religious festivals and other relevant events:

> I'm not participating in organised religious festivals as I used to. I don't go to church on Sunday. I don't go to church for major events as I have been, although that doesn't mean I'm not religious anymore. I am religious as much as before. It's just that I'm much older now and I have my own concepts of God and religion. I have a different concept of God altogether. (Costas)

Yannis, spoke of the internal struggle between his sexual feelings and Christian upbringing:

I have created a more positive image in that I don't fight myself the whole time – not as much as I used to. All the time, it was an internal battle between what I wanted to experience and what society wanted me to experience or the religion.

You know those people that obey the religious teachings, so to speak, and they have a married life, they do so many things that are equally more wrong for humans than what I'm doing. (Yannis)

In some instances, guilt overshadowed any pleasure that might have arisen from sexual activities:

I thought God was going to punish me for being gay. I mean the first time I masturbated, I thought it was really wrong. And I took the Bible out and I held it and I swore to God that I would never do it again. Well, you know, it was my upbringing. (Andrew)

Conclusion

Throughout this chapter I have emphasised the importance of the family and religion in the lives of my respondents. An analysis was provided of how Cypriot men behave and operate through the lenses of two key cultural elements: the concept of women's virtue and the extreme importance of the 'honour and shame' system. They are both entwined and central to the understanding of the coming out process of a Greek gay man. By using extracts from the interviews I tried to give to the reader an appreciation of what a Greek gay man might feel within such a context. The burden of possessing such a powerful secret that could shatter his family is heavy indeed. There will be more than mere disappointment if their son's homosexuality is discovered. The son runs the risk that the family will be shamed and dishonoured beyond repair.

Additionally, the concept of sexuality was examined within the Greek society's context. The polarised and fixed gender structure of the society often hinders the emergence of alternative models of identity for individuals. As a result the Greek-Cypriot homosexuals are left with nothing but clearly defined roles. These roles usually exist within a spectrum of homosexualities rather than one single category of homosexuality in Greek-Cypriot society. The various categories are stratified within themselves and the criteria upon which this stratification is done are both the schema of penetration and the gender role each individual participant assumes. Furthermore, the schema of penetration defines the boundaries in the cultural definition of homosexuality. In other words, a sexual conduct is labelled homosexual or not depending whether penetrative sex has taken place. The strict division of sexual roles (the masculine men, the active and the feminine men, the passive men) among participant individuals seems to perpetuate the myth of heterosexuality as well as that of masculinity. I now move to a discussion of the substantive research effort and to a closer consideration of the data.

Notes

1 My own experience from the army was as follows: After the initial induction period of 40 days we were given two days leave to go home and see our families. Before the Lieutenant in charge handed out the invitations he asked the following: Hands up who is going to the prostitutes this weekend? Needless, to say that everybody raised their hands as failure to do so would indicate a lack of sexual libido and would put into question the soldier's masculinity.

2 'Homosexual' translates the demotic *omofilofilos*, lover (*filos*) of the same (*omo*) sex (*filo*). The term is good Greek but unmistakably a neologism. It is unknown in the classical language. Nor was it originally a Greek invention. Its invention can rather be traced to a German sexologist, who resorted in 1869 to the Greek and the Latin to devise a more scientific and more neutral appellation for a 'condition' that could only be spoken of disparagingly in his native tongue. Thus *Homophilitat* and *Homosexualitat*: in English, 'homosexuality', and in demotic, *omofilofilia* (Pandelidhis, 1982).

3 Again, see Herzfeld, 1985: esp. p.146. The indignity of the mere woman and the attribution of masculinity to her bolder or more heroic counterpart is, however, not simply an aspect of the rural present. Topping finds it well entrenched even in the earliest of Orthodox imaginary: 'Always in patristic writings the male provides the sole measure of worth, virtue and excellence. Celibate women were lauded for their *andriki poni* (manly labours) ...; holy women for their *andrikos loyismos* (manly attitude); women martyrs for enduring persecution and torture *andrikos* (in the manner of men). To become like a man (*andrizesthe*) represented for women the only possible escape from the inferiority of her sex ... The words *yini* (woman) and *thilis* (feminine) acquired such pejorative connotations that in the eulogy for his remarkable sister, St Macrina, St Gregory of Nyssa confessed that he hesitated to call her 'woman' since she had gone 'beyond the nature of a woman' (Topping, 1983, pp.10–11).

4 Loizos and Papataxiarchis (1991b, pp.221–7) offer a different estimation of the *malakas:* '[Malakas] is probably the most widely used term of reference or address in male contexts. Young unmarried men, but often married men as well, greet each other in a joking bittersweet manner by the term malakas, which implies consciousness of a common predicament. It probably suggests the dangers of any attempt to act out sexuality either with unmarried women or with other men. Masturbation, as self-expression, is a kind of safety valve for what are perceived as the 'natural' forces of men's sexuality.'

5 This survey is the only official piece of research ever conducted in Cyprus on the subject of homosexuality. However, two other studies (both conducted in Cyprus) among young people produced the following results:

The first study, was conducted during 1985 using a sample of 741 young people between the ages 16–26. Among other questions, the question 'have you ever had a homosexual relationship?' was asked. A total of 3.0 per cent said yes, while a further 2.3 per cent gave no response. Of this total, 6.3 per cent were men and 0.5 per cent women. Approximately 50 per cent of these were below the age of 16, and a further 34.8 per cent between the ages 17–20. Over a third of these still continued to have homosexual relationships at the time of the survey.

The second study, was conducted in 1990–91 regarding AIDS, under the auspices of the World Health Organisation (Georgiou and Veresies, 1991). A large sample of 3,176 15–18 year old Cypriot schoolchildren were asked about their homosexual experiences. Four per cent of these reported experiencing same sex oral intercourse at least once. These homosexual experiences began from as early as 11 years old up to the age of 18, with majority having their first homosexual experiences when they were between the ages 13–16 years.

6 Similar comparative data can be found in the work done by Coxon and Coxon 1993b.
7 This piece of research was conducted in Cyprus by the Centre of Applied Research in 1994, 1995 and 1997 subsequently. The survey was the first one on 'Cypriot Social Attitudes'. The survey was conducted between 15 March and 15 April in 1994, 1995 and 1997 covering the territory controlled by the Republic of Cyprus.

The sample was drawn among the Greek-speaking population aged 18 and above. The sample was stratified according to sex, district of residence, age group and rural/urban residence. It included 625 people who were interviewed at their home.

The questionnaire covered four major areas of interest:

1 Attitudes on the economy.
2 Attitudes on politics and politicians.
3 Attitudes on civil rights, personal fears and expectations.
4 Attitudes on sexual ethics.

The questions relating to homosexual relations were as follows:

Question 1: What about sexual relations between two people of the same sex (i.e. between two men or two women). Do you believe that this is ...

	1994 %	1995 %	1997 %
Always wrong?	69	65	56
Mostly wrong?	9	13	19
Sometimes wrong?	10	8	10
Rarely wrong?	3	4	2
Not wrong at all?	7	7	6
Don't know/ No answer	2	2	7

Question 2: Do you agree or disagree with abolishing the law that penalises male homosexuality?

	1994 %	1995 %	1997 %
Agree	26	39	41
Disagree	71	61	59

8 See similar work done by Project SIGMA (see Appendix N) between 1987 and 1993. Also see work done by Coxon (1996) and Davies et al. (1993).
9 Question no 6 in the questionnaire reads as follows:

A young 18-year-old boy comes to you in confidence and tells you that he has a sexual relationship with another boy. He finds the relationship rewarding and fulfilling. However, he has heard that it is wrong, and therefore comes to you for guidance and advice. Your advice and guidance would be:

a. To terminate this relationship immediately.
b. To terminate the sexual side of the relationship, but to maintain the friendship.
c. To continue as they are.
d. To visit a Christian therapist.
e. Something else.

Explain below why you would give this advice.

Chapter 5
Methodological Issues

Introduction

This piece of research began as study to monitor the sexual behaviour change and HIV-seroprevalence of Cypriot men resident in London who have sex with men. This turned out to need a primarily qualitative, as opposed to quantitative, study of attitudes and identities in relation to homosexuality, AIDS, and Cypriot culture, particularly considering the significant lack of ethnographic investigation into the homosexuality within the Cypriot community resident in London (see Chapter 1).

In addition, I was interested in the issues of sexuality, double lives, problems associated in coming out, identity per se as well as how these related to ethnic minority gay men. This led in turn to social psychological as opposed to a pure statistical investigation although the use of quantitative techniques was employed in order to analyse some of the findings (see Chapter 6). In particular in-depth interviewing was seen as the primary means of attaining sufficiently detailed and complex information. The process of application of these methods is presented appropriately as a series of considerations before the interview, at the interview setting and after the interview.

Before the Interview: Some Considerations

One of the main issues that I originally considered was of the tape-recording. The question of tape recording interviews is often a contentious one (Brannen, 1988) but particularly so it seems in the case of gay men who do not like to be identified. I have decided from the beginning that I would record all my interviews for the purposes of accuracy[1] and efficiency but I felt strongly that this might not always be agreeable to the interviewees given the intimacy of the information I hoped to solicit and the climate, which prevailed.[2] It is often pointed out that the discussion of one's sex life is second only to the discussion of one's financial circumstances when it comes to sensitive topics (e.g. Bradburn and Sudman, 1979). Any type of 'sex survey' is a difficult topic of research to conduct and usually it might cause a certain amount of embarrassment to the respondent if not to the interviewer (an extensive range of working papers based on the inter-personal relationships between interviewers and interviewees was published by Project SIGMA).[3] If in addition some of the information desired is likely to show the respondent to be in some way 'practising illegal' activities as in the case of unsafe sex then the interview process may not only result in creating anxiety and guilty feelings to the respondent but could place the researcher in a difficult ethical situation.

I have embarked on this project with a clear understanding of the subtext of conversations with gay men about sexual risk. To put it bluntly, part of my interviews were face-to-face exploratory conversations about one's willingness to engage in sexual behaviours that can transmit a painful, stigmatising and fatal illness to oneself or to another man. Aside from the issue of violating perceived social norms within both the gay and straight communities, these conversations may be particularly difficult to pursue in legal jurisdictions where such patterns of risk-taking are regarded by some people as tantamount to murder (especially when engaged in by people who know that they are seropositive).

'Sensitive interviews' also raise important methodological questions since the balancing act in which the interviewer is engaged is that of trading off the 'interviewer effect' with the possibility of gaining additional material through the development of a more intimate relationship with the respondent. The advantages and disadvantages of quantitative and qualitative research were also examined. It was thought that the prospective sample size (certainly less than thirty) would favour qualitative methods. Furthermore, the relative inflexibility of standard quantitative interviewing protocol would probably change and affect the experience sought out in this work.

When it comes to the studying of gay men's sexual behaviour and lifestyle, quantitative methods have not given us a body of theory to guide the interpretation of either the behavioural patterns or of the empirically identified predictors of such patterns. Instead, they have given us descriptions of gay men's sexual behaviour over time, and also they have been used to identify some of the predictions of non-maintenance of safer sex. With the exception of the socio-demographic data gathered in part one of the interview, most of the questions were 'open ended' and sought answers which would describe an experience as opposed to a quantity. For this reason I have opted for the qualitative approach for my interviews. A semi-structured interview schedule was developed to explore the issues outlined in part one (see Appendix).

The reasons why a 'self-complete' questionnaire was not chosen are the following:

- Meeting respondents personally meant that the objectives and rationale behind the research could be explained thoroughly to the subject before commencement of the interview and also granted that questions regarding the use of data could be put to the interviewer. Meeting the individual was important for the purpose of this research as it gave the chance to the interviewer to provide vital reassurances regarding aspects of confidentiality.
- Conducting face-to-face interviews personally is probably the most satisfactory way of ensuring that an interview schedule is (a) completed in full and (b) completed satisfactorily. The meaning of questions that the respondent perceives as ambiguous

can be made clear and the subject further directed where necessary. In addition, responses that the administrator finds ambiguous, elusive or confusing can also be further investigated.
- ... 'The method of eliciting information is more important than the method of recording it' (Pomeroy et al., 1982). The work of Kinsey et al. (1948, 1952), Oakley (1981) and others would seem to demonstrate that (a) by developing a personal rapport with the interviewee, an honesty is encouraged on the part of the respondent which would not otherwise be present, (b) monitoring the responses of interviewees to particular lines of questioning allows the interviewer to be more sensitive to the respondent's needs through flexibility in the sequence of questions – perhaps temporarily skirting those questions which might be causing distress, or by following up and exploring in closer detail those points which seem particularly salient.
- The interviewee can be properly 'debriefed' or counselled in cases of distress and information of a general or specific nature may be supplied, with respondents referred further where necessary.

In particular the last point is important. The possibility of uncovering painful memories or emotions during an interview pertaining to sexual orientation is a real one and the potential reactions of respondents to being probed on these issues had to be carefully considered (Oakley, 1981). The issues of 'exploiting' respondents and then neglecting or abandoning them, possibly traumatised, once the required data has been extracted had also to be considered and to that end interviewees were encouraged to renew contact should they wish to discuss any matter further.

A representative sample of homosexual men is, puristically speaking, impossible to proclaim or produce due to the more or less completely unknown parameters of the population from which the sample comes, despite some extensive studies of sexuality (Kinsey, 1948). Furthermore, any sample recruited according to sexuality is likely to incur questions of definition and, in relation to homosexuality, these more specifically include the distinction of the homosexual person from the homosexual experience, or to put it more exactly, homosexual practices from homosexual identity, and ultimately, the homosexual from homosexuality. There is also a comparative lack of sources or previous study, and certainly no control group

Potential sources for sample recruitment include: Firstly, members of the Cypriot Gay and Lesbian Group; secondly, GUM clinics based in North and South London where the majority of the Cypriot community resides; thirdly, telephone contacts; fourthly gay organisations that happen to have any Cypriot members; fourthly personal advertisements in the local community paper; and lastly, personal contacts through network tracing. The overall difficulty is that of access and of distortion towards the overt as opposed to covert sexualities.

For this research, the following methods were thought of as possible approaches, or at least palliative, to these issues: firstly, the use of snowball sampling as this potentially builds trust, breaks down barriers of access and ultimately forms some cohesiveness in the sample, the problem is that it is limited to repetitions of the same type of people and may often dry up; secondly, the use of informants and contacts to which the same criteria mostly apply; thirdly, the use of personal advertisements in the gay press; and lastly the use of self disclosure and validation as ways of gaining trust.

The means of sampling and recruitment ultimately employed, included:[4] Firstly, the use of snowball sampling from formal and informal contacts; secondly, writing to gay groups and organisations; and thirdly advertising in the gay press. In the end, twenty-two interviews[5] were conducted (n=22) and the details of these are given in the interview schedule in the endnotes.

Interview Setting

Firstly, the interviews were set up through letter or telephone contact and were conducted at the Central YMCA in Tottenham Court Road, London. The use of a study room was provided by the management of the sports club for my use. This venue was chosen because of its convenience and also it would a perfectly legitimate place for somebody to visit without arousing any suspicions. None were conducted in the interviewer's or interviewee's home. Secondly, interviews were tape-recorded to retain information and maintain communication as in conversation with appropriate posture, eye contact and gestures. Interviewees knew that the interviews were recorded in advance either through letter, if used, or on the telephone. None protested, although some said that they were aware of it at first, though not later, and most were unflustered. Thirdly, dress was kept casual, though intentionally not provocative or overly sexual. Fourthly, self-disclosure, particularly prior to the interview, was kept to a minimum so as to control preconceptions and interpreted responses.[6] Fifthly, a social conversation would take place prior to the interview so that the interviewee would relax and feel comfortable with the interviewer and the subject. The contents of that conversation would cover things such as information concerning the nature of the research, what it was for, what would happen to the information, questions of confidentiality and others. The tape-recorder was tested and seating positions arranged for efficiency of recording. Finally, comments and notes were also taken immediately after leaving the interview setting usually in the coffee lounge of the YMCA.

It has to be said that all respondents were first introduced to a common statement of informed consent, which covered issues of anonymity, confidentiality, tape recording and the subsequent storage of data. The interviews themselves were essentially unstructured and the interview schedule itself was broken down into two parts: Part one (see Appendix) consisted of four sections ('socio-demographic background'; 'homosexual identity', 'family life and friends' and 'ethnic minority identity'), which comprised mainly of questions with pre-coded answers. These sections were designed to collect basic data and act as a non-threatening introduction to the interview process. This part of the interview was recorded manually. The second part of the interview was comprised of open-ended questions covering issues of sexuality, coming out, ethnic minority status, homosexuality and double lives. Nine important themes were emerged from this analysis (see Appendix). Interviews lasted from less than one to more than three hours with an average of two hours as I soon realised that more than this was too exhausting for the respondents and myself. Most respondents reported enjoying the interview and many found it useful for exploring personal issues, which they had not previously considered. Interviewees were finally asked if they knew of anyone else who would be willing to be interviewed.

Working from the Inside

Introduction

A number of methodological studies have pinpointed the importance of the differences between the researcher and the interviewee in in-depth interviewing with regards to gender, class and race and the effect these differences might have upon the interview process. In the main these studies have concentrated on the politics and ethics of the social research with gender and race being the dominating themes in most of the feminists' critiques and black analysts' criticisms (Carby, 1982; Phoenix, 1988; Collins, 1990). So far little work has been done on the various assumptions made by the interviewees regarding the sexual and cultural identity of the researcher and what data there are tend to be impressionistic rather than based on a methodological basis (see Chung, 1985; Bhabha, 1990; Hall, 1988, 1991; Project SIGMA). Furthermore, little attention has been given to how the sexual and cultural identities of researchers may shape the research situations when interviewing persons of the same or partially shared racial and/or ethnic and sexual background.

Within this category fall a significant section of the homosexual and bisexual community that is difficult to reach and about whose sexual behaviour we have little substantial or reliable knowledge. This 'hidden population' refers to the category of men from ethnic minority groups who have sex with other men (and often women). Ethnic minority men who are known to have sex with men share common life experiences. They are all exposed to racial and cultural discrimination. The experiences of racism, identity conflict, oppression, and cultural adaptation, as well as the stressful environments, in which these men often live, tend to create a tenacious bond among them – a bond crucial to their survival.

In this section, I would suggest that the unfolding of the researcher's and the interviewee's cultural and sexual identities is central to the ways in which the researcher and the researched position themselves in relation to the 'other'. It is also important if the research itself aims to be both emancipatory and anti-discriminatory. I would also aim to show (see later sections) that any claims of commonalities or differences by interviewees did not necessarily shape the interview process in any predictable or systematic way. On the contrary, such claims were very much contingent upon each moment on each interview.

By providing some examples of my respective interview experiences I shall try and demonstrate the potentially plastic nature of the relationship between the researcher and the interviewee where they share some sexual, racial and/or ethnic commonality. I shall also attempt to highlight the issue of the way in which the interviewer and the research process itself can be used as an emancipatory tool and a catalyst in redefining and renegotiating one's sense of self-identity. This is especially important in research in sensitive areas such as sexuality and HIV/AIDS within ethnic minority groups where the respondents cannot always talk about their experiences and feelings out of fear of discrimination and rejection by the family and the community. These studies show that there are particular problems faced by gay men and lesbians in identity formation, which are not confronted by heterosexuals. The issues highlighted here form the backdrop against which my own research was conducted.

My first name appeared in all the advertisements and leaflets and that enabled the respondents to guess in advance that I was of Greek origin. What they did not know however was whether I was born in London or in Cyprus. One of the first questions that I was asked in the original letter of introduction or during the initial telephone conversation was my racial identity and more specifically my family's residence. That vital piece of information would have indicated to them whether I was classified as an ethnic minority person. Questions about my sexuality were often asked at the beginning of the interview or at different times during the interview, whereas questions about my cultural background at the initial telephone conversation. This was equally important as for all the respondents it was the first time they had the chance to talk about how it felt to be Cypriot and have sex with other men as well. They felt comfortable talking to me.

It was important for me to find the commonalities and work along them rather than try and locate any differences. On the other hand any claims of commonality or difference by interviewees did not necessarily shape the interview process in a predictable or systematic way; such claims were very much contingent upon each moment in each interview. During the interviews I found myself in situations where interviewees either openly or indirectly claimed points of commonality or difference in relation to me, based upon both known or presumed information about me and my life experiences.

Commonalities

Those with strongly held Greek identities were also keen to establish of me 'How Greek are you?', 'Can you speak Greek?', 'Where were you born?', 'Where does your family currently reside?'; all the above served as markers about my own racial background. All the interviews were conducted in English, although I offered to the Greek respondents the chance to talk in Greek if they wished to do so. The language ability (i.e. to speak in Greek) served as a marker of cultural identity during the interview.

Language maintenance is an important aspect of identity and as Taylor and Giles argue in *Language and Ethnic Relations* (1979) language is more than an indicator of ethnicity; it is fairly central to the creation, definition and maintenance of social categories. The fact that a lot of my Greek interviewees could not speak Greek properly made them feel embarrassed and nervous as to how they were perceived by myself. At various times throughout the interview they would throw in one or two Greek words just to show that they had a knowledge and understanding of the language.

However, there were also several ways in which commonalities with me were claimed by those with whom I was talking. The fact that my research was an academic one and I was there to study a subject that has never been studied before gave them the chance to express their dissatisfaction with being Greek or Turkish and sometimes living with their family; all of them have chosen to stress the negative aspects of the Greek/Turkish culture with regards to the tolerance and acceptance of homosexuality.

Furthermore, they have attached to my research work a professional status different from the one that a health authority might have given to it. Academics are well respected in the Cypriot community and enjoy as much status and respect as doctors and religious people do. Their authority carries a certain weight and their work is seldom questioned or challenged. In their eyes I was like a kind of counsellor who was supposed to have all the answers up my sleeve and hence my decision to research the issue of homosexuality in the Cypriot culture. They assumed that I myself also had enough of the way Cypriot people regarded homosexuality and sexuality in general with its double standards and hypocrisies.

They assumed that because I have decided to study this particular social issue in my culture I was starting from a negative position and I was there to criticise it and highlight its drawbacks. As a matter of fact they saw me as a kind of saviour as they believed that my research would finally change social attitudes towards homosexuality in the Cypriot culture.

As one of my respondents said:

> You know very well, Constantinos, and I am sure I am not the only one to tell you this, that Cypriot families can be very suffocating. I have this terrible fear, and it comes from my childhood that my family are going to swallow me up. There is a thing about Greek-Cypriot families where they want to know what you're doing, who you are doing it with, you know what I mean. (Andreas)

Criticism about the hypocrisy of the Cypriot culture towards sexuality and homosexuality together with its double standards was a recurrent feature in the interviews. Those talking to me often made sense of their own identities by laying bare their assumptions about mine. They assumed that I was sharing their hostility towards the way they felt about their families and community. Nobody has asked me whether I was proud about my sexual identity and about being Greek. On the contrary not only did they see me as a professional person but also as somebody who was there to 'spill the beans' to the rest of the world about the drawbacks of our culture.

Another one of my respondents said the following:

> Most definitely, Cypriots have very strong values and one of the strong values they breed into you from the earliest age is that you will have a family one day, children and wife. That thing has been planted into my consciousness from such an age that it's difficult to shift now. I am sure Constantinos, you have experienced the same pressures from your family, haven't you? (George)

Sometimes my sexual lifestyle and preferences, marital status, HIV status, were far more important to them than my Greekness. It was only after I prompted them to think of what aspects in our culture they like most that they stopped and said:

> It's the up bringing. That's one of the many things I like about being Cypriot. You are right; actually, there are an awful lot of things I do like, the hospitality for example. On the other hand, there's the open nature; there's the intrusion into your space, and there's the tactileness and the warmth. The closeness of people. We're very much like Jewish communities in that respect. (Tasos)

Differences

However, when we touched on the subject of racial harassment and discrimination, experiences of commonality could not have been assumed. 'You are lucky for being born and bred in Cyprus'; 'People who were born in Cyprus had a different upbringing from ours'; were common remarks made by my respondents. As a result of that I could not relate to some of the experiences they have described to me. Three of my interviewees have been abused because of their colour and sometimes because of their sexual orientation if they were unfortunate at school and gave away their sexual preferences. I felt I could not help or show a deeper understanding of the situation apart from my usual humane interest.

> I've always felt attracted to boys but didn't know what the word was. I just assumed everybody was. When I went to school I realised it was wrong. I was bullied at school both because of my cultural background and soft nature. I knew then it was wrong but wasn't aware beforehand. I think the other boys at school knew I was gay, they sensed it, I don't know why. No, I do know why, I was more sensitive than they were so I suppose I was an easy target and I never denied it. I was an easy target because I was not English and the discrimination felt even bigger. (Stephen)

> What I am going to tell you now might sound strange to you as you were not born and bred in this country. I am not a racist but I had bad experiences since I was a kid with the English people. It's just a different culture, different way of thinking. Different experience. Me and my Turkish, black and Asian friends sit around and we'll say do you remember when we were kids and used to go round to white people's houses, and they used to say sorry, it's time for Johnnie's dinner now, could you go home please. Whereas if you go round to an Indian household or Turkish household you'll get fed all the time. (Kenan)

> I was speaking to somebody the other day who was Turkish Cypriot and he is thinking of going back and telling his parents. I said it's different for you because you've got a life in this country. You've left your parents there. If I told my parents it would affect my outlook and the way I look on this country. As soon as you get on that plane you've left your parents, left what you've said and come to this country. You can pick up your life. You've always been known in this country as a gay man. Whereas in Turkey you haven't been so just leave it. I think there is a big difference between mainland Turks and Turkish Cypriots. The majority of mainland Turks that come over here don't have an established community. The Greek-Cypriots and Turkish Cypriots do have an established community. You are lucky Constantinos that your family doesn't live here, so you can be yourself. (Kadir)

A further complication arose when interviewing bisexual or primarily heterosexual Cypriot men who happen to have sex with other men. The assumption made here was that I was bisexual/heterosexual myself and that I was enjoying having sex with women and men as well:

> I know I can talk to you because you are a man. I do not like the effeminate gays who are out and about. I like having sex with men like yourself, normal guys you know. (Yiannis)

On the other hand, the positioning of me as someone 'Cypriot born and bred [in Cyprus]' could be suspended when shared experiences of coming out and bereavement issues were being discussed. So when sexual identity was the subject matter, shared experiences could override attributions of me having lived and brought up in Cyprus. A lot of my respondents saw my sexual orientation as a basis for greater mutual understanding. The experiences of being Cypriot and gay were always assumed to be a key point of commonality between the interviewees and me; to acknowledge and recognise this commonality was important in establishing trust and a safe environment between us. It was my responsibility to provide a context within which comments seen as socially undesirable and unacceptable in the outside world are acceptable in the interview setting.

Interviewees' assumptions about my sexual orientation were central in shaping what respondents chose to disclose to me and in what manner. It seemed to me that the more I disclosed about my own sexual lifestyle, family background, coming out, personal relationships the more safe they felt to open up to me. The presumptions about my sexual life when I asked about one-night stands 'everybody does it, don't you', the fact that I shared the same sexual orientation with some of them gave them the presumption that the form of our lives would be the same. How do I explain to them that although the content of our lives might be the same (sexual orientation) the form could be completely different.

Again, when I was discussing drugs with them and more specifically the use of Ecstasy I was asked directly by one of my respondents whether I was taking any drugs or make use of any other substance. When I answered that I have never taken any Ecstasy he showed surprise. Again a presumption is being made that because of my sexual orientation I would have at least tried it. What my research demonstrated was the complexity of these identifications and disidentifications; so many dimensions of sameness and difference can be operating at any given moment. And where two people may claim commonality on one dimension, they may fall apart on another.

Impact on the Researcher

Additionally, the interviews presented a dilemma for the interviewer himself. The fact that I was interviewing Cypriots has brought home to me the different connection that one can have and establish with people from one's own culture. I have been living in this country since 1981 and all my relationships have been with non-Cypriot men. I do visit Cyprus very often because of my family but until the start of the research I was not involved sexually with any Cypriot gay men. Getting in contact with other gay Cypriots has brought home a sense of nostalgia about men from my own culture. Admittedly, for me it was somehow difficult to stay unmoved by their individual stories and personal accounts. The contact that I had with my Cypriot respondents in my research profoundly affected my conceptualisation of cultural identity. These shared experiences (problems of accepting one's sexuality, issues of coming out to the family, dealing with family's pressure in getting married, secrecy, double-lives, mental stress, etc.) encouraged me to get in touch with my Greek identity and brought back a sense of belonging.

It made me realise that I have already started coming home after a long period of inner searching. I have caught myself wanting to defend my culture when the respondents were criticising it. I have found myself wanting to tell them that once the initial period of rejection has passed they would realise that there is still love among family members. I have already experienced what they were going through. It was more of a case of wanting to say to them 'Don't worry, it's going to be fine in the end. You are a lovable and a good person irrespective of your family's reaction towards your sexuality'.

Their experiences served as a reminder to me how far I have travelled and what I have experienced and made me realise how fortunate and blessed I am to arrive at this point and doing research on a topic that has caused me so much pain and difficulties in the past.

Issues of Sampling

Introduction

Sampling issues for surveys of members of such high-risk groups (e.g. gay men, bisexuals, i.v. drug users, and prostitutes) and their behaviour pose severe challenges. These groups constitute what are termed hidden[7] populations in the sampling literature. The main challenge in sampling a rare population is to find economic methods for obtaining the sample, a challenge that is made more difficult in the present context by the social stigma associated with membership in these high-risk groups. The groups are not only rare but, because of this stigma, they also tend to be hidden, so that their members will not be readily identified by other people. The following section discusses a range of techniques that may be used for sampling rare populations and consider their applicability for surveys of ethnic minority gay men. A more detailed analysis of the data as collected from the questionnaire and the open-ended questions can be found in Chapter 6. The probability sampling techniques are discussed first.

Probability sampling Kalton (1993) identifies eight different techniques under this section as:

1 Screening
2 Disproportionate stratification
3 Multistage sampling
4 Multiple frames
5 Multiplicity sampling
6 Two-phase screening
7 Location sampling
8 Snowballing

In addition to the above one a more recent probabilistic approach will be examined namely the random walk strategy (Klovdahl, 1976). This approach is more directly relevant to sampling rare populations.[8] It is not the purpose of this chapter to provide an in-depth analysis of each one of these techniques. However, the snowballing and the random walk strategy will be discussed in the following paragraphs.

Snowballing (link tracing) The key idea behind this technique is that members of some rare populations know each other. The technique is applicable only for rare populations for which this condition holds. Snowballing works by first identifying some members of the rare population, asking these members to identify others, asking those so identified to identify yet others, and so on. Snowball sampling provides a relatively inexpensive way of generating a sample of a very rare population provided that the members of that population know and are willing to identify each other. Snowball sampling is, however, a nonprobability sampling procedure, and that carries with it a number of limitations.

Firstly, with snowball sampling, members of the rare population who have many contacts with other members of that population have greater chances of being selected for the sample than those with few contacts, and those who are socially isolated from other members of the rare population have minimal chances of selection.

Secondly, there is the question of whether this procedure would provide useful sociological information (Klovdahl, 1976). The answer to this question, presumes knowledge about the social networks in the gay Cypriot community resident in London, which was not available, and, accordingly, a definitive answer was not possible.

Thirdly, the fundamental theoretical assumption of social network theory which is the assumption of connectedness (e.g., Simmel, 1955; Barnes, 1954; Srinivas and Beteille, 1964; Blau, 1967) does not seem to hold either in this case. It would be quite unlikely to find many isolated dyads, circular relationships, or perfect cliques in the gay Cypriot community.

It would appear that for the above mentioned drawbacks snowball sampling would not be advisable for sampling gay or bisexual Anglo-Cypriot men for the purpose of this study and that snowball estimates would not provide very much useful sociological information about the respondents concerned.

The random walk strategy A useful category for studying urban social networks appeared to require the use of a social survey approach in conjunction with some form of probability sampling (Klovdahl, 1976). This design was to involve selecting a person at random from a large population, interviewing the person to obtain (among other information) a list of persons linked to the initial respondent by social relationships of a specified kind, randomly selecting one of the persons so listed to be the next person interviewed on the 'random walk' ('through' a large urban social network), and so on, for the desired number of steps, with the procedure being repeated for the number of random walks desired. Again some problems might arise as the technique assumes that the population is easily accessible and identifiable. In the case of the gay Anglo-Cypriot men that strategy would pose an initial problem in persuading the initial respondent to identify (if any) another Anglo-Cypriot man who has sex with men.

All probability techniques are based on a series of assumptions that when it came to the 'hidden' population of the Anglo-Cypriot men seemed to collapse. These assumptions are next discussed:

First, the target population for the survey needs to be precisely defined: for a survey of gay men in a certain city, the meaning 'gay' needs to be clearly specified to meet the survey's objectives, the boundaries of the city need to be clearly identified, and the time of the survey needs to be specified.

Second, ideally the sample size should provide every gay man in the target population with a known, nonzero, probability of being selected for the sample.

Third, data should all be collected from all the gay men who are selected for the sample.

After careful consideration the probability sampling techniques were thought not to be appropriate for constructing a sampling frame of Anglo-Cypriot men resident in London who have sex with men. All methods seem to be costly and they were subject to a component which causes a major bias in sampling. It is for these reasons that the non-probability techniques were then considered in designing a sampling frame in dealing with issues raised in this book. These are discussed in the next section.

Non-probability techniques These have enjoyed an enormous growth over the last number of years. The disadvantages is the nature of the link because it has been repeatedly found that the attempt to snowball within a category ignores the links that are across and not within. There is no particular advantage in categorised or controlled snowball sampling and that is why this research project first choose the Cypriot men and then questions them. The assumption that a lot of the surveys make when it comes to gay men's behaviour is that often a given gay man's friends and acquaintances are of the same age-relationship (Davies et al., 1993) type as himself and therefore information about someone of the same type would be easily available. Also they put them in categories first and then interview them. People's networks are far removed from that. The main problem with all probability and non-probability sampling techniques when applied to hard-to-reach populations is the cost practicality.

Given the budget and time constraints I was confronted with I had decided that neither of these two approaches would serve my purpose. That left me with the only feasible option but to adopt a convenience egocentric network approach. In other words I needed to find my sample first and then carry out a series of in-depth interviews.

Conclusion

In this chapter I have attempted to convey something of the multi-faceted reality of doing research with people of the same or partially shared ethnic and sexual background. As a researcher I was surprised to see the extent to which my sexual and cultural identity was directly or indirectly questioned or commented upon by respondents. More attention needs to be paid to the assumptions that interviewees made about the sexual and cultural identity of the interviewer and examine how and in what ways these assumptions affect the unfolding of the interview: the interviewees may disclose certain kinds of information based on their assumptions about the researcher (social desirability effect); they might decide to give their personal accounts and describe their life stories and identities in terms which compare themselves to assumptions about the researcher.

Commonalities and differences are inter-changeable throughout the interview process. Markers of cultural and sexual identity such as language fluency, place of birth, family's residence, coming out to the family, being in a relationship, living with a male partner, can be the bases for claims of either commonality or difference. I would argue that such claims were very much contingent upon each moment in each interview and it is only when each interview is examined separately and individually that some of the debates about sexual and cultural identity and the research process can be further explored in any depth.

Notes

1   That was particularly important when AIDS-related issues were discussed with the respondents. The advent of this epidemic has raised and continues to raise challenging

new issues-legal, ethical, and practical-that require ongoing critique and reflection about human subjects research should be conducted (Gray et al., 1995).

Additionally, I was careful when it came to obtain the respondents' truly informed consent at the beginning of the interview. I did recognise that a simple signature on a form was not enough. I made sure that each participant must truly comprehend the research in which he was participating and consent with full knowledge of possible risks. As a researcher examining issues of sexuality, which covered HIV and AIDS, I was aware of the various interests at stake and the conflicts among them-for example, my ambitions, the public's interest in learning how to manage the epidemic, and the risks faced by research participants.

2 The use of a tape recorder does not mean that the interview can become less attentive to what is being said. This is important regardless of whether a standardised open-ended interview format is being used or the more informal, conversational approach.

One's full attention must be focused on the interview. One must be thinking about probing for further explication or clarification of what he is now saying; formulating probes; linking up current talk with what he has already said; thinking ahead to putting in a new question that has now arisen and was not taken account of in the standing guide (plus making a note at that moment so one will not forget the question); and attending to the interviewee in a manner that communicates to him that you are indeed listening. All of this is hard enough simply in itself. Add to that the problem of writing it down even if one takes shorthand in an expert fashion-and one can see that the process of note taking in the interview decreases one's interviewing capacity. Therefore, if conceivably possible, tape record; then one can interview (Lofland, 1971, p.89).

3 The acronym SIGMA represents Socio-sexual Investigations of Gay Men and AIDS. Project SIGMA is a longitudinal, non-clinic based, serological and behavioral study of the sexual and social lifestyle of gay and bisexual men in England and Wales. (It is also part of the English study under the auspices of WHO Global Programme on AIDS Homosexual Response Studies.) SIGMA is one of the larger cohort studies in Europe and the only study in the U.K. to have emerged from the gay community. Funding for the project began in 1987 until July 1994 from the Medical Research Council and the Department of Health. To date, the Project has interviewed over one thousand men, half of whom have been interviewed five times at [median] intervals of ten months. The main aims of the study are to describe the sexual behaviour and lifestyles of gay and bisexual men; to monitor changes in sexual behaviour in relation to HIV/AIDS; to examine attitudes to different sexual behaviours and relationships; to investigate reactions to safer sex practices; to estimate prevalence of HIV and other viral infections in a non-clinic group of gay and bisexual men.

Since July 1994 the original Project has dispersed and re-grouped with two different academic centres. The first group, called 'Project SIGMA, Essex' has had funding from the Medical Research Council for a series of studies on Ethnic Minority Groups, Gay and non Gay-Identified bisexual men and Young Gay Men. The second group, with research workers at Portsmouth and Brixton is called 'SIGMA Research' and concentrates on studies of male prostitutes and health and needs assessment primarily of gay men. Project SIGMA uses several complementary methods of obtaining information, including:

- The detailed structured interview in which each respondent is asked for detailed information on sexual history and current practices (centered upon the Index of Sexual Behaviour [Coxon et al., 1992]), numbers and characteristics (but not names) of sexual partners, health, and attitudes towards HIV and safer sex.

Methodological Issues

- The sexual diaries (Coxon, 1988) are a daily record of sexual activity kept by respondents for a month after each interview. So far the Project has collected information on about thirty thousand sexual encounters, which allows a unique analysis of their structure.
- Blood and/or saliva samples are also collected at the interview by trained staff and tested for HIV-1 antibodies and other viral markers. Results are available to respondents through trained counsellors.
- The postal survey of sexual behaviour is a self-completion questionnaire, which appears in the gay press periodically.

4 The chronology and full details of the sampling methodology are as follows:

Initial Contacts – Summer/Autumn 1994

The following were met personally by myself to volunteer people as potential interviewees:

Andrew Billington; Adviser/Councellor – James Pringle House
Dilip Lakhani; Health Adviser – Guy's Hospital
Roz Pendlebury; Chief Executive – Landmark
Robert Canner; Adviser – GMFA
Terry Blair; Health Adviser – Health First
Murad Kutay; Adviser – Health First, Health Promotion, Lambeth
Dr David Tomlinson – St. Mary's Hospital
Dr Patrick French – Middlesex Hospital
Dr Faizal Samji; GP – Shepherds Bush Centre
Peter Tovey; Adviser – London Clinic, Whitechapel Hospital
Vivien McDonald; Manager – Kobler Centre, St. Stephen's Clinic
Dr Shean Waldron; St. Mary's Hospital
Necip Varan; Social worker – Health Promotion Unit
Mustafa; NAZ Project
Paul Young; Outreach worker – King's College Hospital
Robert Lee; HIV and AIDS coordinator – St. Ann's Hospital
Dr Philip Kell; The Archway – Whittington Hospital
Lesley French; Health Adviser/Councellor – James Pringle House
Kyriakos Spyrou; Health Adviser – Harringey Council

Groups/Organisations – Summer/Autumn 1994

The following groups and organisations were written to for interview volunteers. Additionally, copies of my advertisement were sent to the perspective managers of these organisations for distribution.

The London Lighthouse
Royal Free Hospital
The NAZ Project
King's College Hospital
The Mortimer Market Centre
iCARE – Islington Community

The Archway Sexual Health Clinic
St Ann's Hospital
Body Positive
Crusaid
Terrence Higgins Trust
CARA
LADS

Advertising – Summer/Autumn 1994

An advertisement for volunteers was placed in *Capital Gay* for one month, in *Gay Times* for three months and *Boyz* for one month. Also it appeared in the local community paper *Pariaki*.
The interview schedule of sources was as follows:

#1   Andreas (*Boyz*)
#2   Andrew (*Boyz*)
#3   George (*Boyz*)
#4   Georgis (*Boyz*)
#5   John (*Boyz*)
#6   Kadir (*Pink Paper*)
#7   Kenan (Snowball from CHAN)
#8   Kostas (*Boyz*)
#9   Lou (*Gay Times*)
#10 Michael (*Boyz*)
#11 Mike (Snowball from CGLG)
#12 Nick (Mortimer Market)
#13 Oz (*Boyz*)
#14 Stephen (*Gay Times*)
#15 Tasos (*Capital Gay*)
#16 Yerasimos (Snowball from University)
#17 Costas (*Boyz*)
#18 Tonis (Snowball from CGLG)
#19 Michalis (Snowball from CGLG)
#20 Lefteris (Snowball from CGLG)
#21 Yiannis (Snowball from CGLG)
#22 Fotis (Snowball from CGLG)

The following people initially contacted me for an interview but subsequently changed their minds or did not show up at the interview:

#23 George (*Gay Times*)
#24 Jim (*Capital Gay*)
#25 Panos (*Boyz*)
#26 Stephen (*Boyz*)

Age of interviewees	Age
#1 ANDREAS	32
#2 ANDREW	29
#3 GEORGE	31
#4 GEORGIS	33
#5 JOHN	21
#6 KADIR	36
#7 KENAN	26
#8 KOSTAS	31
#9 LOU	28
#10 MICHAEL	27
#11 MIKE	31
#12 NICK	33
#13 OZ	29
#14 STEPHEN	31
#15 TASOS	41
#16 YERASIMOS	22
#17 COSTAS	26
#18 TONIS	34
#19 MICHALIS	34
#20 LEFTERIS	24
#21 YIANNIS	42
#22 FOTIS	27

Occupational distribution

PROFESSIONAL	16
SELF-EMPLOYED	2
STUDENTS	4
TOTAL	22

Place of birth

CYPRUS	4
ENGLAND	18
TOTAL	22

Educational qualifications

SECONDARY	22
UNIVERSITY/POLYTECHNIC	11
OTHER HIGHER EDUCATION	7
OTHER	5

6   Interviewees would usually assume the sexuality of the interviewer via the nature of the interview. This information was not usually volunteered. However, if asked I was honest and answered simply.
7   A hidden population is characterised by a low prevalence of its members in the general population and by the difficult access to its members as well (Spreen, 1992).
8   A rare population is characterised by the low prevalence of its members with a specific trait in the general population and by the relatively easy access to its members (Spreen, 1992).

Chapter 6

The Gay Greek-Cypriot Man in Britain: A Profile

The Research Issues

The lack of research on Anglo-Cypriot men who have sex with men has precluded highly focused work within a particular zone of 'gay Cypriot' issues and has resulted in research parameters being set wide enough to give meaning to a general exploration of the domain. In part one of this book the following eight questions were highlighted for investigation:

- Disclosure or nondisclosure of gay identity to their families.
- Cypriot cultural factors in acceptance of gayness.
- How do gay Anglo-Cypriot men negotiate a path through their two worlds to avoid their coming into conflict, and what is the result when they meet?
- Activism and participation in the Anglo-Cypriot and gay communities.
- Choice of community (Anglo-Cypriot versus gay) in which individuals felt more comfortable.
- Self-definition of identity.
- Perceptions of discrimination because they are gay or Anglo-Cypriots or because they are both gay and Anglo-Cypriots.
- What are the effects of the 'double life syndrome' on i) the general psychological well being of the Anglo-Cypriot men, ii) their ability to form and maintain personal relationships

Of these issues, some have been dealt with in Part One of this book. Some others have been touched upon using anecdotal data transcribed from the interviews. No statistical data has yet been presented however, and no detailed analyses offered (A breakdown of basic sample socio-demographic data may be found in Chapter 5). In this chapter, I propose to look more closely at the above questions beginning first with the disclosure of gay identity.

Disclosure or Non-disclosure of Gay Identity to Their Families

Results from the research indicated that most respondents have 'come out' to someone in their family. A sibling, usually a sister, was overwhelmingly the first person in the family to whom my respondents had 'come out' (Davies et al., 1993). Although 72 per cent (n=16) have 'come out' to a family member, however, only seven respondents (31 per cent of the sample) have 'come out' to their parents. When one takes into account that 6.2 is the mean number of years this group has been 'out', the percentage of respondents who have 'come out' to their parents seems low. In addition, almost all respondents reported that they were 'out' to most of their friends. It seems then that there are specific cultural values defining the traditional roles, which help to explain the reluctance of Anglo-Cypriot gay men to come out to their parents and families.

In 1989, Tremble, Schneider and Appathurai reported on a study of three lesbian and seven gay Canadian young people from Greek, Asian, Portuguese, Italian and Indo-Pakistani cultural backgrounds. Of some interest to the following discussion of coming out to the family are two points made by the researchers.

First, parents often do not understand what it means to be gay or lesbian, and the idea of homosexuality is often especially difficult for them to understand. Some parents are unaware that gay men even exist, and when faced with the concept, may believe that their gay son want to be a woman. Another common misconception is that the son's homosexuality has been caused by the dominant culture, which is viewed as decadent, and that he has been seduced.

Second, gay and lesbian youth:

> Will be most in conflict with their cultures when religious beliefs are orthodox, when there exists a strong expectation to reside with the family until marriage, and to get married and have children, and when gender role expectations are polarised and stereotypical. Paradoxically, these values also provide the pathway to reconciliation between homosexual children and parents. When the love of children and the value of family ties are strong, nothing, including homosexuality, will permanently split the family. (Tremble et al., 1989)

Tremble et al. also note that although there may not be a complete understanding, and positive feelings may continue to be absent, the focus on sexual orientation will eventually lessen, as will the conflict between parents and their gay children. Often, the parent-child relationship will remain intact, bound by love.

In the case of Greek-Cypriot families living in England, I would submit that parent-child relationships often return to the level Welts (1982) describes as being loving and loyal but somewhat superficial, with parents discouraging deeper connection and children (whether adolescent or adult) colluding in the maintenance of such dynamics by not talking about their feelings or concerns. For these families, love and loyalty are the qualities most valued, and as several of the cases in this research demonstrate, families often avoid discussions of homosexuality (both prior or subsequent to coming out) so as not to pit love and the family's *philotimo* directly against each other.

Sometimes a son will use the smallest of lies to avoid reminding a parent of the 'shame' he feels but keeps hidden. Greek parents believe that it is their duty to teach their children what is 'right' even if that means the lessons can be learnt only through a process as painful as rejection. Other Greeks would view these parents as 'paying the ultimate sacrifice' in order to teach their children properly, and as executing their parental duties with honour.

The following story describes the pain that George went through when his mother decided to cut any communication with him for a whole year, after he has come out to her. Its importance as an account justifies its length. He told me:

> When I came out to my mother it was very difficult. The first thing she said was 'you're destroying your life, you're destroying our lives'. Then I would ring at home and she would never answer the phone or the answer phone would be on – or my dad would ring and say, 'She's got a headache', or 'She's gone to the toilet'. That lasted for a year'. Yes! I don't know how we managed to do it. She did manage to do it and not to actually talk to me. She wrote to me horrendous letters, the most unbelievable letters. I used to just tear them up. They were really terrible letters. They used to make me feel so upset and horrible. That was very painful. So that was very painful really. I only saw her once that year in Athens, when I went on holiday. She made sure that there was someone else around so that she could kind of keep it all on the surface and all of that. Well I hated her and I told her that I hated her. You see I wrote back horrible letters. I used to tear them up and then I used to reply to them using the same tone, emotional blackmail as well. And basically I told her what I felt like when we talked about those years of being left with my grandmother, and how I felt that wasn't the way to bring anyone up basically, you know. And I said that you say that you feel so much pain, what do you know, and all that crap. And I made clear that she knew the pain that I had been through basically. Also, not just from not coming out, but also from being alone and not being with family, you know, all of that. We went through all of that so we went through all of that. All of these letters obviously got worse and worse and deeper and deeper. She must have realised what I had been going through and that it wasn't just a phase, to use a cliché. Of course, the first thing she said was that it was Robert's fault. I had been led astray and all that. (George)

If we were to ask his mother, however, why she did not welcome him back into the fold, she would likely say it is out of great love for him and would reject the notion of its being 'punishment'. George himself says that if his mother were to invite him back, she would believe that this implied her acceptance of his homosexual orientation.

One must emphasise that not all Greek-Cypriots living in England behave according to Greek cultural scripts. Again, the degree to which a family has assimilated to the dominant 'Western' culture will likely play a significant role in how family members view and experience one member's coming-out process. With equal caution, I should note that it is important to remember that many Greek-Cypriots in England strongly identify with their Greekness, even though they may be several generations removed from immigration.

In some cases disclosure of one's sexual orientation might cause family friction and subsequently damage close family relations:

> I wouldn't say I had ideal parents, far from it, but I still very much love them and I don't want to hurt them, basically. Also they are very old and they would never understand about my sexuality. (Andreas)

In the following example, one can see that the family relations are damaged because of lack of honesty among family members. John talks about his pain and frustration by not being able to share his life with his parents whom he is very fond of. As a result of that, he finds himself more and more distant from them. He told me:

> It's bad but they [the parents] are definitely losing me. Ever since all that big fuss we haven't really spoken about anything remotely personal, except for my mum saying why don't you get a girlfriend but apart from that there just isn't that closeness. I don't feel close to them at all. If it's somebody's birthday, Easter or Christmas I will go home but only because I feel I should, if I had the choice I wouldn't go. If I don't visit regularly they start saying you don't love us any more, I love them just as much if not more than they love me. They seem to think I can only love them if I am in the same room as them. If I am in Brighton then I don't love them, don't want to be with them. (John)

Sometimes, the response from a parent when confronted with the sexual orientation of his/her son can take the form of a panic attack. In the following example, Andrew's mother did not know how to react and her only concern was the neighbours' reactions. Additionally, she suggested going and visiting a doctor who might happen to have a cure. Andrew's story unfolds in the following lines:

> She went into the Greek 'Oh, *Panayia mou* (Oh, My Virgin Mary) you know, 'What are the neighbours going to say? Oh my God, what am I going to do? I'll take you to the doctor. We'll go to the doctor, I'm sure he's got an injection ... O.K. He'll give you an injection'. I started laughing. I said 'Mum, the doctor wont be able to, like, you know, make you straight'. 'Who is it? Who is it? It's that Michael, isn't it? Don't you ever bring him into the house again'. The thing is, Constantinos, from the time I told her to two minutes later, she changed completely, different colour, I mean she was practically holding on to the breakfast bar. She was about to collapse and I thought, 'God, what have I done?'. (Andrew)

In some instances the outcome was successful. The following two examples, show the parents have not rejected the respondent and the parent-child relationship has remained intact. At the very least, the parents have reached a personal understanding of their son's sexual orientation that, distorted or not, enables them to come to terms with it. Although a complete understanding and a positive feeling may not exist, sexual orientation is no longer a constant focus of attention and conflict.

> On the positive side, I think the closeness that I feel with my mother, the fact that I can laugh with her and that she can laugh with me and we joke and we can go shopping together. This is off the record. If a mother was going to go shopping with her son, let's say, and she would pick up a bra, would she say 'What do you think of this colour?' to a straight son? She wouldn't, would she? We connect. There's a connection that's there. I know my mother

doesn't have it with my brothers. She's almost like fearful of them, because they're very much like my father, in mannerism, in attitude, in mentality. So I think if it wasn't for my mother, I wouldn't be happy being gay. The fact that there's someone that close to you, who acknowledges that you're gay, but doesn't talk about it, I think it helps, it does, and it makes you feel good about it. (Kostas)

Oz's mother, although from a working class background and of little education, has been understanding and supportive. He said:

When I came out to my mum I must have been about mid-twenties. It was very difficult. I was surprised because she was very calm and emotionless because by this time she had worked herself up that something was very wrong, so me saying that to her, it wasn't what she expected. It wasn't as bad as she thought it was going to be. I could see she was a bit confused but she was glad it wasn't something like death or a major illness. She was quite calm; she said if that's what it is we can deal with that, it's not a problem. By this time I was quite emotional and I was crying, she was really calm, the opposite of how I was. She said I want you to come round, nothing has changed. She said to me how can you meet people and I explained there is a whole community of gay people. I gave her a general overall view. When she did ask a few questions they were more sexual orientated than friendships. In her eyes as in a lot of her generation all she wanted for her kids was to be happy and in her eyes for us to be happy means to be married, have kids, a husband, a car, that type of thing. So she couldn't understand how I could be happy. She didn't know how two men could settle down, have a relationship. (Oz)

Cypriot Cultural Factors in Acceptance of Gayness

When respondents were asked to describe the Anglo-Cypriot perception of gay Anglo-Cypriots, nearly all the respondents agreed that there was a denial of existence of Anglo-Cypriot gay men. This supports the idea that homosexuality is commonly perceived by ethnic minority groups as a 'white, Western phenomenon'. Furthermore when asked whether 'they find it easier or harder to come out to other Anglo-Cypriots' 20 respondents (91 per cent) thought it was harder because homosexuality is such a taboo in the Cypriot culture and that they felt neither accepted nor acknowledged by other Anglo-Cypriots. In contrast, the two (9 per cent) respondents who thought coming out to Anglo-Cypriots was easier indicated that they felt this way because they felt other Anglo-Cypriots would understand what being part of a minority group was like and would feel sympathetic. As might be expected, these two respondents identified more strongly with being Cypriot than with being gay.

Assuming a similar importance of family and community relationships in Cypriot cultures, it is likely that Anglo-Cypriot gay men have not 'come out' to their parents because of the overwhelming fear of rejection and stigmatisation. In order to understand the experience of a Cypriot gay man's coming out process, we first need to understand the socialisation process of young Greek boys and girls in general and the role of (heterosexual) men and women in the Cypriot culture. As Nicolas Gage (1989) puts it: 'From birth a Greek girl is groomed for her wedding' ('How can I marry you like that?' a Greek mother will invariably shout at a female toddler who has soiled her clothes). Everything that happens after a Greek woman's wedding day is anticlimactic except the birth of her son' (p.153).

Greek is a culture of rigidly maintained family and sex roles (Welts, 1982). The husband/father's authority is ultimate and unquestioned. Wives and daughters are expected to comply with this patriarchal authority. Young girls are socialised early to understand that their brothers are held in higher esteem and that their brothers' activities are more important than their own (Callinicos, 1990). The role of a daughter is to obey and to support the efforts of the male members of her family in preparation for the day she marries and has a husband of her own. The expression *Eisai kalo koritsi* (You are a good girl) is commonly repeated from childhood to adulthood to those who dutifully fulfil their role expectations, which include helping their mothers by learning to keep a clean house, how to cook and sew, and how to be good hostesses. Thus a young girl grows up associating her 'goodness' with serving men and, in this way, honouring her family. Children are expected to obey instruction and not to express their own needs, wishes, or opinions (Welts, 1982).

Whereas Western culture views adolescence as a typically stressful time and as a time when the adolescent begins to individuate from family, Greeks view adolescence as simply a part of the natural evolution of development whereby individuation occurs within the context of family (Pappajohn, 1988). Paternal authority still is not challenged. Instead, children learn to emulate their parents, progressively taking on more sex role-appropriate responsibility within the family and, through this process, developing their sense of increased maturity. Welts (1982) offers the following observations:

> Since Greek parents discourage dialogue with children, adolescents rarely turn to their parents to discuss their thoughts, feelings, or changing life values. Contact remains loving and loyal but somewhat superficial and ritualised around meals, holidays, and family gatherings. (p.278)

Offspring will always remain 'children' no matter what status or professional achievements they attain. They will be expected to honour advice given freely by the older generation. This attitude contrasts with cultures where children are better educated than their parents and parents acknowledge their achievement by accepting their grown children as peers (p.277). If one parent is widowed, the children are expected to take in the surviving parent. Daughters are expected to take care of ageing parents (p.278). The family structures of the research participants reflected the commonality of such living arrangements. Sixteen of the participants had their grandmothers or grandfathers living with them for some portion of their childhoods.

To understand further how women have been viewed within Greek society, it is informative to examine some of the anthropological literature focusing on a feminist analysis of gender, such as the work of Ortner (1974), Dubisch (1986) and Seremenakis (1991), who all discuss the concept as 'polluters'. This is the notion that women have the capacity to be powerful polluters (and thereby 'destroyers') of the environment and yet, as Dubisch notes, they are also capable of controlling that pollution. Basically women are viewed as being closely associated to 'nature' (because of their natural processes, such as menstruation and childbirth), whereas men are closely associated with 'culture' (because they are the creators of social order). In this model, nature and culture are viewed to be in opposition. In many societies culture serves to control or regulate nature; culture is valued over nature, and by association, women's status is viewed as subordinate to that of men. Furthermore, in Greek culture, female expressions of sexuality (another natural process) outside the context of marriage also pose a threat to social order. A common Greek expression to describe an adulteress is to say that she is deceiving her husband in the street. The street is where dirt and trash exists. It represents the outside 'wild', compared to the home, which should, by Greek standards, be the picture of cleanliness and order. In short, it is every woman's responsibility to exercise the modesty and shame necessary to control her sexuality, along with the strict control that male guardianship provide (Dubisch, 1986).

Penetration can be as much about power, then, as intimacy. Loizos (1994) gives the following example from his field notes to support the fact that men in the Greek culture use penetrative sex as a form of domination and discipline over their wives:

> The leader of the Greek nationalist anti-British underground in my village rejoiced in the nickname 'Yeros', the Old Man. Two of his younger adjutants later, after independence, stopped following his political lead, and were known to support a different leader from his own favourite. This was related to tensions at the national level, which were only with difficulty contained in the village. Someone said something witty about this and it was repeated for days afterwards in the coffee shops: 'The Old Man should have fucked his two lads, and then they would have listened to him'. At first I thought this was some veiled hint about the Old Man having homosexual preferences, but men explained patiently that this was not the point at all: men have sex with [*gamoun*] their wives, and wives obey them. So, had he treated them like wives, he would not have had disciplinary problems. In their own words my informants were implying that Yeros would have been a super-male, which has echoes of Lacan's notion of the 'Phallocrat'. It appears from this that to discipline is to feminize; to have penetrative sex with someone is to discipline him, and thus to feminize him. (Loizos, 1994)

In some villages there are still men who share the belief that a woman would always find the first man to take her virginity irresistible and, significantly, able to command her for the rest of her life, even if she married another man. 'Small wonder, then, that the men wanted to marry virgins, and small wonder, too, that I heard men discussing striking their wives occasionally, as if it were a routine matter of imposing a husband's authority, and nothing remarkable' (Loizos, 1994). On one occasion, such a discussion concerned whether or not it was reasonable for a man who came home late to wake up his sleeping wife and insist on having sex with her whether she wanted to or not.

Opinions differed. One man felt it was somewhat unreasonable, and if the woman was not willing, she had a right to be allowed to sleep. Another man said, with a laugh, that, if he found himself in this situation and his wife refused, he would be inclined to fetch her a couple of blows (*na tis doko ena-thkio mbattsous*). 'But not heavy ones', he added, and he laughed, and the other two men laughed' (Loizos, 1994).

It seems from the above that in the context of interpersonal relations, to be a dominant man can imply the use of force to subdue or discipline someone else, and neither the other person's gender, nor the physical weapon (a penis, a fist) need to be distinguished. Beyond the religious and sex role socialisation factors that serve as the backdrop to understanding the Greek gay man's coming-out process, there are two key cultural elements that are very much entwined and central to an understanding of this process: the concept of women's virtue and the extreme importance of the *philotimo* in a Greek person's life (Dubisch, 1986; Kennedy, 1986). *Philotimo* literally means 'love of (one's own) honour'. The *philotimo* is to be guarded at all costs. The following passage from Nicolas Gage's book *A Place for Us* (1989) illustrates the meaning and importance of the *philotimo* in a Greek person's life. In a conversation between Gage and his father, his father says:

> But before I die, I want to tell you that I'm proud of two things in my life. The first is all you've done, and the second is that none of my daughters ever shamed me. For that matter, even my nieces – all the Gatzoyiannis women – they've all been virtuous and never once dishonoured our family.
>
> ... I blew up at him. 'What's so important about that?' I snapped. 'Why is your pride and the family honour based on the virtue of its women?'
>
> 'You don't think that honour is important?' he asked me in a tone that intimidated me despite my anger.
>
> 'Yes, honour is important!' I replied. 'But it should be based on what we each do as individuals, not on the sexual propriety of our women relatives. In most families some girl is going to step out of bounds. Does that mean the entire family has to lose its good name and respect?'
>
> 'To me, my friends and my enemies – yes!' he thundered. 'All the men I grew up with lived in fear that one of their women would shame them. You could wake up one morning and find out that everyone you knew looked at you differently because some girl in your family did something crazy. That's why I'm proud that none of my daughters, none of the women in the whole family that bears our name, brought shame on me. I can walk with my head high before any man I know.'
>
> I decided to drop the argument ... but his words helped me understand both his thinking and the societies I encountered in Iran, Iraq, Pakistan and Turkey, where women were oppressed and carefully guarded by men but carried within themselves the knowledge that they had a weapon that could shatter their entire family in a moment. (p.408)

Now, imagine what a Greek gay man or lesbian might feel within such a context. The burden of possessing such a powerful secret that could shatter the entire family is heavy indeed. There will be more than mere disappointment if their son's or daughter's homosexuality is discovered; he or she runs the risk that the family will be shamed and dishonoured beyond repair. Greek girls are taught from an early age that they should never lose their virtue (i.e., their virginity), as it is directly tied to the family's *philotimo*. In the northern mountains of mainland Greece, there are a number of villages, such as Naoussa and Souli that have statues or songs commemorating the courage of their women for 'dancing to their graves'. As folklore has it, these women threw their babies and their other children off the cliffs and then, one by one, danced themselves off the edge rather than fall prey to the Ottoman-Turks during their struggle for Greek independence (1821–1827), and face probable rape and slavery. The community norms are such that their mothers cite these mass suicides and martyrdom to daughters as examples of the importance of women protecting their virtue and honour. The lesson is one of death before dishonour. As Gage (1989) notes, 'A wilful daughter can ruin a man and his descendants for all eternity'(p.86).

Whether a Greek man is gay or heterosexual, because the *philotimo* is so important he has learned at a very young age to make use of lies and deception to cover up any shortcomings or unacceptable behaviour, because, after all, nobody is perfect. The Greek word for 'lie', *psema*, does not have the overtones of moral failures found in English (du Boulay, 1976). Kennedy (1986) notes that Greeks see lying as more socially acceptable than telling the truth if the truth goes outside social norms. So what we have is a culture in which the individual 'cares deeply about maintaining the appearance of honour' (Kennedy, 1986, p.138). Dishonour comes not so much from breaking the rules as from being caught (Dubisch, 1986).

An illustration of such collusion between parents and gay sons is found in the following cases:

> My boyfriend every now and then would come down to London and stay with me. He'd sleep in my bed and I'd sleep on the floor and one night I said to my mother 'Oh mum, I can't sleep on the floor any longer, I'm going to sleep in the same bed as Michael, because I can't be bothered'. She said 'O.K. that's fine' and she came in to say 'Goodnight' to us, and she looked and then said 'Goodnight' and she looked at Michael and she said 'Oh, my daughter-in-law. (Andrew)

Michael believes that his mother knows about his sexuality and she tries to let him know through little things, like the following:

> I think my mum probably knows. The people who usually call me at home are all men and ex-boyfriends. No women have called our house and asked for me over the last few years. Also a T-shirt I had that wasn't mine, it was my flatmate's and I brought it home and it got washed and it was one of those Tom of Finland's T-shirts. She just left it on my bed. (Michael)

In some cases the individual lives with his partner in the same house then the partner is presented as his lodger. This was found to be common among my respondents. George commented:

> My dad knows there is something going on. He knows that Robert is my lodger, of course, he knows Robert well. We have been together for seven and a half years, so you've got to be stupid not to think, not to allow it to cross your mind that this might be your son's lover, you know. I go on holidays with Robert. (George)

For some others, their actions speak louder than their words. Andreas told me:

> One is that my behaviour is not that stereotypical Greek. The other is that I haven't got married yet and I don't date women, so they can't be that stupid, though they probably think that I am going through a phase, you know what they're like. (Andreas)

John is certain that his mother knows after reading his diaries:

> Yes, my mum definitely knows. No question, she has read my diary. I used to keep a diary and it had accounts of blokes that I'd met, blokes I'd been out with. (John)

The emphasis and value placed on maintaining the appearance of honour go a long way in explaining why English Cypriot gay men are so invisible within the Greek community and to one another. Further obstructing the Anglo Greek gay man's outreach toward other Greek gay men is the historical/cultural legacy mentioned previously – that of being socialised into believing that only within the family can safety and trust truly be relied upon. Illustrative is a common Greek proverb: 'Do not ever confide your secret to your friend; for he will tell it to another friend and then it will be your misfortune' (Bucuvalas, Lavrakas and Stamatos, 1980).

As one of my respondents said:

> It's connected, going back to relationships and not having the confidence. I've had it drilled into me, especially recently since I've been at university, you can't trust your friends. Family is the only people that are going to be there for the rest of your life. Even though I know what they are saying isn't true, it does affect you subconsciously. You do, I am very cautious, even with my closest friends, even though I tell them everything, every now and then you think, well maybe I shouldn't trust them. I am hardly at ease with my self. (Michael)

Andreas faced the similar experience:

> As you very well know Cypriots have very strong values, and one of the strong values they breed into you from the earliest age is that you will have a family one day, children and wife. That thing has been planted into my consciousness from such an age that it's difficult to shift now. So it's always there nagging me. They also tell you from an early age that the only people you can trust is your family and no one else. I used to be wary of people but not anymore. (Andreas)

For some others, the sense of duty towards one's parents proves to be a heavy burden even at the expense of the individual's own happiness and well-being. As Mike said:

The main reason I haven't come out to my mum is because it would kill her. Even though we're not close, yes, my mother has sacrificed her life for me. She was the one who was getting beaten up by my dad, she was the one who had to go out to work to feed us – to say to her 'Yes, I am gay' that would totally destroy her. I do love her, but it's not the intimacy that I would like to have. Sometimes I have the feeling that I am sacrificing my own happiness for her. I know it might not be fair but it's a case of, like for any Cypriot son or daughter, it's a duty. They've looked after you, that's the way I see it, now it's my turn to look after her. (Mike)

Negotiation of Two Worlds

The question now arises of the relative prevalence of the 'exclusive' versus the 'paired' double life against that of those men who are 'fully integrated'. One hundred per cent of respondents admitted either disguising their orientation or passing at some time in their lives. It has already been noted that 73 per cent of respondents (n=16) were employing passing or disguising techniques. Seventy-three per cent were living exclusive double lives within their families. Sixty-four per cent (n=14) of this number made regular visits to the gay scene and were open to other gay men about their sexual orientation. The other two expressed their dislike of the gay scene and all they prefer to socialise in straight social circles. Since it has already been noted that the figure of 73 per cent also represents respondents who were systematic disguisers to their families, and since there were no instances of exclusive double lives in the homosexual realm (that is, no Cypriot man was out in the family whilst still disguising on the scene), it can be seen that those respondents who were systematic disguisers within the family were always disguisers within the community. This point will be examined in more depth in the following section.

I will offer two examples here:

I live with my boyfriend in the same house for the last ten years. They see him as my lodger. And they're fine, you know, but they still ask me, you know, 'When are you going to get married?' 'How long are you going to stay with that man?' I don't think I'll ever tell them. I just like things as they are. It's something that we don't discuss. Last time she asked me 'Well aren't you ever going to get married?' I said 'Maybe after I'm forty or never'. (Kadir)

Kenan realises as he grows older that his family does matter to him and tries very hard to keep a balance between the two worlds. He said:

The older I get I've started to become more aware of my family and I've just told my sisters that I'm gay and that didn't go down too well. I used to think what I'll do as a young person is fuck my family, never see them again, get on with my life. The older I get I realise I don't want to do that because I actually do love my family. I'm considering it to come out to my family. If they don't know that I'm gay there is a lot of me they don't know. (Kenan)

On the other hand, Lou is quite happy with the status quo of the situation as long as his mother doesn't bring up the subject. He said:

> I don't think I will ever tell them because you have a family and if you do then it's fifty per cent they are going to accept you and fifty per cent they are going to reject you. If they reject you then you lose all that loving, caring thing; and I don't want to lose them. It is my family. If I lose them I don't know what is going to happen. If things are running smoothly right now and I don't have any problems with them why change them? Stupid isn't it? (Lou)

In some instances, little white lies seem to be the only solution. Michael told me:

> No I don't think I can talk to my parents, not at all. Yes, I have to lie to them sometimes. I've got no hang ups about it. It's obviously better, just small lies like who I'm going out with or where I'm staying for the night. You see, my family is very important to me and I do love them. (Michael)

George, however, thinks that a little diplomacy wouldn't harm anybody. He argues that by employing the 'keeping mum' technique the family relations are kept in balance. He said:

> I think my Mum suspects. The problem is that I am very close. I don't think I will ever tell them about my sexuality as that would hurt them very much. I guess I have to accept the fact that as a gay Cypriot person I have to protect my family. My father has heart problems. I couldn't never do this to them. They adore me. I adore them. Well, it's diplomacy really. I don't think it is an out straight lie and it's not the honesty, it's a diplomatic way of keeping them happy and keeping myself happy. For example, I do have girlfriends, I do go out with girls but I don't sleep with girls. (Georgis)

Stephen hopes that the support he would get from an understanding lover would enable him to negotiate the path in order not to come to any conflict with his family.

> Yes and my family and my sexuality are important to me. I don't see why you should choose between the two, I think you can have both but obviously if my parents knew if I was gay it would make things very difficult. I suppose what I expect from another man is consideration and patience. They don't know anything. There isn't anything to know because I am not living with anyone. That's it, as far as I'm aware they don't know anything. Also I'm not living at home, I've always kept my private life private so I wouldn't change that and I wouldn't want to hurt them so I wouldn't tell them. If I ever have a boyfriend I would show him to my parents but wouldn't say this is my boyfriend, I would say this is a friend of mine. Perhaps I would introduce them or maybe not. It is not easy but I don't want to hurt my parents, I would rather hurt myself. Which is why I need a boyfriend who can understand that and if they wouldn't then it would just be more pressure on me. I couldn't get involved with somebody who had very fixed ideas. (Stephen)

Three Different Communities

Introduction

In the previous paragraphs I have focused on Greek-Cypriot gay men in the context of coming out to self and to family. At this point, it may be beneficial to step back and review criticisms that have been raised about theoretical assumptions and coming-out models as they stand today. First, as Greene (1994) has noted, of all the clinical and empirical research on gay men and lesbians that has been published, most has been conducted with white, middle-class gay men and/or lesbians, and therefore lacks generalizability to gay men of colour. As Greene states, the literature does not 'take into account the realistic social and psychological tasks and stressors that are a component of a gay and lesbian identity formation for men and women who are of a visible ethnic minority group' (p.390). Factors such as racism and discrimination, and their effects on the well-being of gay men of colour, are much too significant to ignore. In addition, Greene notes that the cultural heritages of gay men of colour may include vastly different views regarding men's roles and homosexuality from those of the dominant culture.

In addition to the above, I would argue that another problem exists with the psychological literature regarding gay men: Researchers in England and the United States seem to treat the white race as if it comprises simply one monolithic ethnic culture. It is falsely assumed that all white English and Americans espouse the values of the dominant white (Anglo-Saxon Protestant) culture. Just as we cannot generalise most of the existing research to gay men of colour, it would be inaccurate to assume that these findings are generalizable to all white gay men. It is indeed a rare study that inquires into or reports the ethnic backgrounds of its white gay men subjects. Many studies, however, try but do not succeed in gaining large samples.

Furthermore, most American studies have systematic information on ethnic minorities unlike some of the British studies. I suspect that most of the research has been conducted using a subject pool that consists of those who primarily belong to or identify with the dominant culture because these are the men most likely to be 'out' and, therefore, identifiable and available to be studied. Less likely to be out and available for study would be white gay men who also belong to cultures that are less tolerant of homosexuality, for example, Orthodox Jewish people such as those living in a concentrated Jewish community in Hendon, London; members of the Portuguese or Maltese community; those who are Asian, Russian and Serbian. Greene (1994) states:

> An understanding of the meaning and the reality of being a man of colour who is also gay requires a careful exploration of ... factors. These factors include the nature and importance of the culture's traditional gender role stereotypes and their relative fluidity or rigidity, the role and importance of the family and community, and the role of religion in the culture.

But these same factors need to be considered in any attempt to understand the meaning and reality of white gay men whose self-identity is highly related to an ethnic culture that is viewed as 'different' from the dominant one, and even more so when religion is strongly embedded in that culture. This is not to say that ethnically identified white gay men don't live in, identify with, and even accept many of the dominant culture's values as their own. At the same time, however, they likely have not relinquished their ethnic identities and those identities' concomitant values. Perhaps the simplest way to understand this is to consider the difference between 'assimilation' and 'acculturation'. This has been extensively analysed and covered in Chapter 3. Often researchers are mistaken when they blur the distinction between race and ethnicity and treat them as one and the same.

Choice of Community

We now turn our attention to coming out in the community. when asked about their social networks, twenty of the research participants (91 per cent of the sample) replied that they socialised mostly with non-Greek gays. When asked if they were out to any Greek people other than family, only four said they were, but none (n=0) of these men were out only to other Greek gays. Furthermore, when asked, 'In which community do you feel more comfortable (Anglo-Cypriot or gay) and why?', the respondents (n=20) who chose the gay community gave the following reasons:

Double standards basically. The Greeks would help you to succeed but when you succeed they going to back stab you. (Lou)

I have more in common with gay men than with straight Cypriots. (Kadir)

All I want is to be happy and somewhere nice to live. A boyfriend and a job that I enjoy. I don't think I can find all the above in the Geek culture. (Michael)

So, I never had too much contact with my own culture. When I did have contact with it, I disliked. I would love to learn my own language and love to learn my culture. (Mike)

As Greek-Cypriots they think they are far better than anyone else. I am sure they look down on me because I don't have a house and I'm not married. They are close minded, they think there is only one way to live a life. An unwillingness to be open minded. (Stephen)

I think I'm proud, I'm proud of the women in my family. I despise the men. I think that's generally how it goes. So I'm very, I'm proud to meet Greek-Cypriot people who have pride in themselves; I don't want anything to do with Greek-Cypriot people who are kind of like, who have got this kind of peasant mentality. I can't bear it. It's surprising how strongly I feel this, now you talk to me about it, because it's, you know, it's almost like connected to a class thing. (Nick)

Cypriot society works, on gossip. Basically there is family that has got no gossip about them and that's my mum, two sisters and me. There is no gossip about us and everybody is very jealous. My sisters are aware of the fact that they are just waiting for a slip up and that worries me. (Kenan)

Those who felt more comfortable in the Anglo-Cypriot community (n=2; 9 per cent) explained:

The closeness of the family and the support you may be getting if you are in trouble. I relate to myself as a Greek person first. (Georgis)

The hospitality and the way we perceive life and people. My culture and beliefs as indeed Greek. (George)

I suppose knowing what they want in life. Being ambitious and hard working. Having a set of values, I think they [Cypriots] would be more faithful than maybe an Englishman would be. (Stephen)

Yes, a lot of my thinking is influenced by my upbringing. The competitiveness is still there. The fact that I show a lot more initiative than English lads in a work environment comes from being Cypriot. I'm very glad, in many respects that my background is Cypriot, because a lot of English attitudes, I cringe. (Tasos)

However, it is interesting that although these men remain closeted within the Greek community, this does not seem to extend to the gay community. In fact, twenty of the men were involved in gay rights activism as self-defined by participation in gay pride marches, participating in several charity functions and being involved with AIDS hospices and organisations. Considering the degree of press and camera coverage such events often bring, this is far greater visibility than one might expect from Greek gay men living in London. All participants' families live in London. Regardless, several noted that although they worried over being 'found out', either by a parent to whom they were not out or by a family acquaintance who might be watching the news and feel compelled to gossip, all felt it was important to follow through.

As Fassinger (1991) notes, most of the existing models of gay identity development, such as Cass' (1979) widely cited model, have a linear and prescriptive flavour implying that developmental maturity rests on an immutable homoerotic identification as well as a positive public (and often political) identity. The models are insensitive to diversity in terms of race/ethnicity. The unfortunate implication is that non-political acceptance of one's gay identity is seen as a form of developmental arrest (Fassinger, 1991, p.168).

Thus I would propose that it is indeed an interesting juxtaposition that occurs when one tries to apply Western models of coming out to beliefs surrounding the development of a positive gay identity of a Greek man living in London. On the one hand, an argument could be made that as a group, the twenty-two gay men in this study still possess a fair degree of internalised homophobia and shame, as some are not out to one or both of their parents, six are out in the Greek community, and most worried about being shunned or that their families would be exposed to hurtful gossip (damaging the *philotimo*, thereby shaming the family). Yet, by another measure, many appear to have gone beyond merely 'accepting' themselves and are on the far end of the continuum of 'outness, advocacy, and celebration', even by Western standards.

Self-definition of Identity

To determine whether respondents differentiate between feeling a part of a community and acknowledging their own personal identity, respondents were asked which terms they used to identify themselves and which part of their identity (Anglo-Cypriot or gay) they more strongly identified. Results indicated that the two concepts (community identification and personal identification) are similar for the respondents. The sixteen respondents (73 per cent) who used the term 'Anglo-Cypriot gay man' to identify themselves answered that they identified more strongly with the gay part of their identity:

> I also have this terrible fear, and it comes from my, my childhood, that my family are going to swallow me up. There's a thing about Greek-Cypriot families, which is so suffocating where they want to know what you're doing, who you're doing it with. And when I was fifteen, I managed to break away because I got involved in Theatre, which was something none of them knew about. And it was like my refuge and it's remained my refuge. I have no dependence on my relatives. (Nick)

> I would choose to say that I feel gay and then Cypriot. The thing that bothers me now is that I am not a fulfilled person. Once you've come out to the family and they can accept it, which I know mine won't, at least you can bring a boyfriend home to meet the family. My problem is not with the gay life but with my own cultured life. That's the difference. (Mike)

> No, I think Manchester is what did it for me. I think it was quite an important factor, moving away because a lot of Greek-Cypriot gay men don't leave home. They stay at home, obviously the parents want them to stay until they get married or whatever. They don't have an opportunity to do that and think I was lucky but it's not a question of luck, it's a question of being strong enough to leave home and being desperate enough. That's probably what made me the person I am now, leaving at that age. I left home a different person to what I am now. Now I can go and live at home and things like that don't bother me. I've changed, stopped blaming my parents for things, and separated myself from them whilst I'm living with them. I feel much closer to the gay community than the Greek community. (Michael)

In contrast, four respondents (18 per cent) who said that they identified themselves by the terms gay Anglo-Cypriot and reported that they identified more strongly as Anglo-Cypriots made statements such as the following:

I identify as a Cypriot man first because similar backgrounds and experiences are stronger bonds for me than sexual identity. Sex comes and goes but to have a solid ethnic identity is important. (Costas)

I would say, that my Greekness defines who I am. I am first Greek and then a gay man. My sexuality may change one day but my Greekness still remains intact. (Georgis)

Yes. I would say that I am proud of being Greek and gay. I want to socialize with other gay Greek men as we understand each other much better that any other English gay man would. It's different. If I have to choose I would say I am Greek first and then gay. (Fotis)

However, two of my respondents (9 per cent) refused to choose between the two identities. They reflect the reality that most Cypriot gay men feel most complete when they can be accepted as being both gay and Cypriot, as the following comments indicate:

I identify as being both. Why can't we marry the two [being gay and Greek-Cypriot]. I wouldn't like to choose really. Both my culture and my sexuality are equally important to me. (Stephen)

Both communities are not mutually excluded. I think one complements the other. The Greek community supports my Greekness while the gay community supports my being a gay man. (Kostas)

I believe both identities are important to me. I love the Greek music, the theatre, and the arts. As a matter of fact I love anything that is Greek. But at the same time I love men. For me there is no distinction. (Tonis)

These results suggest that, when a choice of identification is required, more respondents identified themselves as gay than as Anglo-Cypriot but that others refused to choose because it would mean denying an important part of their identity. It is likely that each person determines for himself depending upon the stage of identity development he is in, whether it is more comfortable to be Cypriot among gay men or gay man around Cypriots or whether both are intolerable and he must be acknowledged as both Cypriot and gay by everyone. As we have seen in Chapter 2, identity development can be a fluid and ever-changing process and as a result of that an individual may choose to identify and ally more closely with being gay or Anglo-Cypriot at different times depending on need and situational factors.

Discrimination Because of Race or Sexual Orientation

Another factor examined during this research was whether or not respondents had been discriminated against because of their race, their sexual orientation, or both. The majority of the respondents (n=14; 64 per cent) reported that they felt more frequently discriminated against because they were gay than because they were Cypriots. Only one respondent (n=1) felt discrimination because of his race. Some others felt that they experienced more discrimination overall because of being both Cypriot and gay, what Wooden et al. (1983) termed a double minority status.

The following two examples, illustrate the discrimination two of my respondents experienced because of their sexual orientation.

Stephen believes that the bullying he faced at school had an impact upon his late acceptance of homosexuality. He remembers:

> I can remember being accepted at the age of ten at an all boys comprehensive school [name withheld]. I remember being very happy because I knew I was gay then so I must have known before. I've always felt attracted to boys but didn't know what the word was. I just assumed everybody was. When I went to school I realised it was wrong. I was bullied at school both because of my cultural background and soft nature. I knew then it was wrong but wasn't aware before hand. I think the other boys at school knew I was gay, they sensed it. I don't know why. No, I do know why, I was more sensitive than they were so I suppose I was an easy target and I never denied it. I was an easy target because I was not English and the discrimination felt even bigger. (Stephen)

On the other hand, Nick found it hard to hide his attraction towards boys at school. He said:

> I think that boys understood my vulnerability and capitalised on it. So that boys, I think, straight boys, who knew I was gay, would kind of try and get their rocks off by getting me to make love and I wouldn't. I had a rough time at school and I try not to remember those days. (Nick)

Kenan, however, felt discriminated because of his race. He too remembers:

> What I am going to tell you now might sound strange to you as you were not born and bred in this country. I am not a racist but I have had bad experiences since I was a kid with the English people. It's just a different culture, different way of thinking. Different experiences. Me and my Turkish, black and Asian friends sit around and we'll say do you remember when we were kids and used to go round to white people's houses. And they used to say sorry, it's time for Johnnie's dinner now, could you go home please whereas if you go round to an Indian household or Turkish household you'll get fed all the time. I never felt welcomed at my English friends' homes. I sensed that for some reason I was not really accepted. It was only after I have grown up and started realising the discrimination between black and white that things made sense. (Kenan)

Effects of the Double Life Syndrome

Relationships

When it came to personal relationships the effects of leading a double life can have a negative and stressful effect on the individuals involved. 50 per cent (n=11) of respondents who had experienced 'steady' relationships felt that their situation effected either:

- The prospect of a satisfactory relationship.

    Sometimes, I feel that I am destined to be on my own. I would like to find a partner but I don't think anyone could put up with my family. There is so much pressure. Every time I meet somebody I end up finishing the relationship first out of fear in case my family finds out. (Lefteris)

    I used to go out with a really nice guy but the pressures [not being out to my family] has split us up. In the beginning he was understanding but after a while he couldn't cope. (Yerasimos)

- Their partners:

    My partner has a lot of patience. He would like to me to come out to my family but I can't. Sometimes he gets angry with me and I can understand why. (Fotis)

- The quality of relationship with their partner:

    I can't let him answer the phone in case my mother phones. She still doesn't know that he lives with me. (Georgis)

    It's difficult to give them one hundred percent if you have to exclude them from all the family functions and events. I make up a story every time I want to go on holidays that a different friend comes along with me. (Costas)

Those who were single (n=12) would like to have met a male partner and form a relationship. They would prefer somebody from their own culture but their prejudices and misconceptions made them believe that it was extremely difficult to find such a Cypriot man. They had a negative image of other gay Cypriots. They claimed that most of them are very effeminate. Therefore, they turned to the mainstream gay scene in order to find potential partners. Those who were in a relationship admitted that it would have made a difference to be with another Cypriot man but due to the reasons mentioned above they have formed relationships with men that they have met in the mainstream gay scene. Of the twenty-two men I have interviewed, only one had ever dated a Greek man. Some of the reasons why a lot of respondents have a difficulty in forming relationships with their other Cypriot men are expressed in the following extracts:

At first, I thought it would be really nice to meet another Cypriot. They're far and few in between, and the Cypriots that I did meet, they were all queens, very camp, very, very camp. And I couldn't really take that, being very camp. (Andrew)

It would be ideal for me. Looking in the Greek-Cypriot community in London is not the right place to look for a Greek boyfriend. Maybe in Greece or Cyprus, but here in London they are with their families and they are scared. It makes me hate Cypriots. (Michael)

I would like to be with a Turkish lover. I think there is a difference between an English lover and non English lover. He doesn't even have to be Turkish Cypriot, he just has to be somebody who isn't white European. I'm not being racist, I'm not. It's just a different culture, different way of thinking. Different experiences. (Kenan)

For George, having a relationship with a non-Greek man made him believe that assimilation within the British society would become much easier:

But you see, at that point I wanted to get away from my culture, my identity. I mean I spent years pretending I wasn't Cypriot, not that I ever told anyone I wasn't Cypriot but I spent my time denying it. I just wanted to get away from that identity, away from what it meant, for someone who is gay, and also, because I wanted to assimilate myself in British society. (George)

Similarly, John tried to disassociate himself with the Cypriot culture. One way was to have relationships with English men. He stated:

No I wouldn't like to have a Greek lover. It's all part of the disassociation with everything that is Greek. I'm not really attracted to Mediterranean men. I prefer English men, French and English. I like dark haired people but I've only ever had sex with two Cypriots. (John)

For Stephen, it is a matter of learning something different from another culture other than the Greek. He believes that an English partner would offer him the things that he lacks within the Greek culture. He said:

I don't want to go out with somebody who is similar to myself. I want to go out with somebody who is different, say somebody who is English, much more positive. They are different but the chances are they would have had a different upbringing, more positive about being gay, more sure of themselves. To inspire me in a way and give me confidence, not someone who is in the same position as myself, that wouldn't help me because we would both be trying to hide. I would like to be with somebody who is very comfortable with whom he or she were and to help me. That's what I found working in television and with other gay men, they were all, most of them were English, they were very strong, got involved in all the marches, they were very proud of being gay and you won't find Greek-Cypriots who are like that. (Stephen)

In addition, his ideal partner should have an understanding of the difficulties and pressures that Stephen is facing within the family. He went on to say:

I suppose I am attracted to opposites in a way but I would expect them just to have a bit of understanding, they don't have to like the situation, just to understand. Most men that I've fancied were English. I suppose I like blonds, you tend to go for the opposite type to yourself. It's something about the way they are brought up, they are more at ease with themselves. I think they could teach me more than maybe I could learn from other Greek-Cypriots. (Stephen)

Mental Health

Some of the psychological effects of leading multiple existences were examined in chapter two. At least eight of the respondents (36 per cent) experienced 'nervous breakdown' and suffered stress as a result of their attempts to keep both family and their private lives apart.

Stephen said:

I was very depressed when I was growing up. Especially when I realised it was wrong to be gay. I did try to commit suicide. I don't know if it was because I was gay or because I was unhappy, probably a mixture of both. I started seeing a counsellor. I've only recently stopped. I was on and off tranquillisers but they didn't help. At the end of the day the problem is still there. You are torn between family and your true self. (Stephen)

As a result of the stress I was going through I suffered some kind of physiological condition, where I would be breathless. So that's why I sought help from this psychiatrist that I saw a number of occasions. Yes, I would say I had a nervous breakdown a few times ... (Andreas)

Yes, there have been a couple of times when I have thought about committing suicide but never actually tried it. The last time I thought about it was last Friday. I started getting upset about that and also I started thinking about relationships and I thought if I had somebody with me it wouldn't matter as much. Then I thought I couldn't say anything to my mum or dad so I felt very alone and was thinking out my suicide note in my head but didn't really get much further. It was things like thinking what is the point of me being at university? I do want to do it for myself but a good part of me doing it is to make my parents proud and I think what is the point. I could get a first and once they find out I'm gay that will be it so I get depressed about that as well. It's all very deep. I had a bit of a breakdown about eight months ago, not a breakdown it was more a crying fit. Yes, I'm constantly depressed. Just started crying for about an hour. About $1\frac{1}{2}$ years before that I got really depressed about my parents not accepting me and I wrote in my diary that my mum read that I'd thought of committing suicide. But I don't have the guts, even though they say it's the chicken's way out, coward's way out, I don't even have the guts. (John)

Results of the Questionnaire

From the survey data, a series of themes were emerged relating the third section of the questionnaire, namely ethnic identity and sexuality. This data is summarisable as follows:

1   **Disclosure of gay identity to family:**
    Yes   73% (n=16)
    No   27% (n=6)
    1.1 **Disclosure of gay identity to parents:**
         Yes   32% (n=7)
         No   68% (n=15)

2   **Easier or harder to 'come out' to other Anglo-Cypriots?**
    Easier   9% (n=2)
    Harder   91% (n=20)
    No difference   Nil

3   **Negotiation of a path between the two worlds:**
    'Out' as gay in the Anglo-Cypriot communities but not 'out'
    as gay in the heterosexual community   Nil
    'Out' as gay in the heterosexual community but not 'out' in the
    Anglo-Cypriot community   82% (n=18)
    'Out' both as gay in the Anglo-Cypriot community and in the
    heterosexual community   9% (n=2)
    Not 'out' either as gay in the Anglo-Cypriot community, or
    as gay in the heterosexual community   91% (n=20)

4   **Choice of community**
    Gay   91% (n=20)
    Anglo-Cypriot   9% (n=2)
    Both   Nil
    Neither   Nil

5   **What do you consider to be your identity?**
    Anglo-Cypriot gay man   73% (n=16)
    Gay Anglo-Cypriot   18% (n=4)
    Neither   Nil
    Both   9% (n=2)

6   **Experienced discrimination because of being Cypriot?**
    Yes   5% (n=1)
    No   Nil
    6.1 **Experienced discrimination because of being gay?**
         Yes   64% (n=14)
         No   36 (n=8)

7   **Effects of the double life syndrome:**
    7.1 **Caused stress and break-ups in relationships:**
         (11 respondents were in relationships at the time of the interviews)
         Yes   50% (n=11)
         No   Nil

7.2 Caused mental health problems
Yes   36% (n= 8)
No   64% (n= 14)

Given the analysis on the effects of the double life syndrome as examined above, the finding that 36 per cent of the sample had experienced some form of depression gives cause for some concern, and one is bound to ask whether or not such a figure is generalisable to the wider population of Cypriot gay men living in London. I would suggest that such a figure is unlikely to be accurate. The disclosure patterns for the wider population are almost certainly dissimilar to those of the sample population due to the fact that the research sample i.e. twenty-two Cypriot men resident in London who have sex with men is unlikely to be representative of the large number of non-heterosexual Cypriot men living in London. There are some 70,000 Cypriots living in Greater London, several thousand of which are likely to be other than heterosexual. At the time of writing, the CGLG's (Cypriot Gay and Lesbian Group) membership stands at between fifty and seventy and is unlikely to rise above a couple of hundred, even with the new advertising taking place these days. Thus, only a minority of people who would seem to be more politically orientated, confident, and 'out', are likely to volunteer for interview than those who have not yet come forward. The remaining 'invisibles' may never become part of the group nor respond to advertisements like mine for research within the Cypriot culture on sexual matters for several reasons. They may not hear of the CGLG's existence, or its activities may not interest them. However, it is the researcher's belief the main reason is that the idea of coming out in the Cypriot community, let alone approaching an 'out' organisation such as CGLG, is inconceivable. For this reason, my guess/estimate would be that the national (but unverifiable) percentage of those living double lives and suffer various forms of mental depressions and psychological problems is substantially higher than is to be found with the sample of this book. The inbuilt tendency to under sample those with deep anxieties regarding their dilemma then means that this research offers only conservative estimates of the difficulties faced by Cypriot men who have sex with men. This, however, is a problem intrinsic to the nature of the sample as opposed to the size of the sample.

The difference between the sample and wider population, although serious in terms of generalisability, is not uncommon when researching non-heterosexual populations. When sampling from pubs and clubs or otherwise enlisting the assistance of individuals whose sexual orientation can be prima face established, one is sampling a specific and highly pre-selected section of the desired population and one which is almost certainly not representative of the larger, non-visible population. It is therefore unlikely that many of the results of this research could safely be generalised beyond the sample examined for the purposes of this book.

Conclusion

The results from this chapter indicate that the self-identification of gay Anglo-Cypriots is reflected in several factors: choice of community identification, choice of terms (Anglo-Cypriot gay man versus gay Anglo-Cypriot), situational factors such as whether they had disclosed their gay identity to their families and the Anglo-Cypriot community, and their own perceptions of how they are perceived by the gay community. Results also indicate that the majority of respondents identified more strongly with their gay identity than with their Anglo-Cypriot identity, although there were several respondents who insisted on acknowledging both aspects of their identity as Anglo-Cypriots and as gay men.

In terms of the Model of Homosexual Identity Formation (Cass, 1979), most of the respondents in this study reflected identities of Stage 4 (Identity Acceptance) and Stage 5 (Identity Pride), because they generally accept and are openly proud of their gay identity (with some exceptions of nondisclosure to parents). In terms of the ethnic Minority Identity Development Model (Atkinson et al., 1979), most of the respondents reflected strong Anglo-Cypriot identification and are in Stage 4 (Introspection) and Stage 5 (Synergetic Articulation and Awareness).

Because most of the respondents were selected from advertisements in the gay press and thus may identify more strongly with being gay than with being Anglo-Cypriot, these results may not be generalisable to a larger Anglo-Cypriot gay population. Further studies might include a more random sampling of gay Anglo-Cypriots, as well as use of extensive quantitative analysis methods, more comprehensive interviews with a larger sample, or both.

Finally, some implications for understanding identity development can be derived from the results of this chapter. The results suggest that the extent to which an individual identifies as Anglo-Cypriot gay can depend on several factors, including the perceptions of homophobia in the Anglo-Cypriot community, perceptions of racism in the gay community, disclosure or nondisclosure of homosexuality to family and community, and affiliation with the Anglo-Cypriot and gay community. Identity development is an ever-changing process, and individuals may base their with one identity or community on their changing needs for support as well as on desires to share cultural factors. Some of these needs are met better by other gay men, some by other Anglo-Cypriots, some only by other gay Anglo-Cypriots. Ideally, it seems that individuals who have double and triple minority status feel most complete when they can acknowledge and be accepted for each one of their identities as gay, as Anglo-Cypriot, and as men.

Chapter 7
Epilogue

Introduction

In this final chapter I will begin by addressing those concerns which are outstanding or which have so far escaped consideration. Specifically, I want to begin with a brief note on the make-up of the sample itself before moving to a consideration of the notion of dichotomies within the Greek culture. The role of 'coming out' as a solution to role strain is then considered and some possible drawbacks emerging from this analysis are offered. Finally, a general portrait of the 'ethnic minority gay man' is presented before concluding with some thoughts on the future of the Cypriot gay man in London and Cyprus itself.

A Note Regarding Sample Non-Homogeneity and Other Inherent Shortcomings

Some inherent shortcomings of this research also need to be mentioned:
Firstly, three of the respondents in this research were under twenty-three years of age and although in a minority, such individuals' experiences were found to differ from those of the older respondents in an important respect, namely, that those individuals who have been involved with the gay community for a long time lived and experienced life under very different circumstances. The circumstances of their lives made plain the inadequacies of the questionnaire, since many of the questions regarding outings to gay bars/clubs, an open gay lifestyle etc. simply did not apply. It must therefore be recognised that the views and opinions of the majority of interviewees in this study are unlikely to represent young Anglo-Cypriot men less than twenty-three years of age.

Secondly, it has already been remarked that the experiences and problems faced by Anglo-Cypriot gay men living in the countryside may be qualitatively different from those in urban areas like London. Yet without sufficiently large numbers of provincial Anglo-Cypriot gay men to match a sample for the purposes of a valid comparison a more accurate analysis of experiential contrast cannot be undertaken.

Thirdly, an analogous but more serious problem was posed by the non-existence of a female lesbian population within the sample. Realising that the possibility of making a valid comparison between the male and female 'gay Anglo-Cypriot' could be equally dubious, the potential for an important differential meant that the territory could not be so easily ignored. It would be interesting to do research among Anglo-Cypriot lesbians and explore key cultural concepts and relevant historical factors that may be converging as forces in the development of an Anglo-Cypriot lesbian identity and in the coming-out process.

Fourthly, more research is required to find out whether Greek-Cypriots in London (first and second generation) share the same beliefs and attitudes towards sexual and social issues as the Greek-Cypriots in Cyprus. A report published in April 1998 by the Centre of Applied Research,[1] Nicosia, Cyprus (Cypriot Social Attitudes, Survey 1997) showed the following results:

- 20 per cent of the respondents believe that it is wrong or almost wrong for an unmarried man to have pre-marital sexual relations. On the other hand, 45 per cent of the respondents believe that is wrong for an unmarried woman to have pre-marital sexual relations.
- 80 per cent of the respondents believe that it is wrong for a man to have extra-marital affairs. When it comes to women, 88 per cent of the respondents believe that it is wrong for a married woman to have extra-marital affairs.
- 74 per cent of the respondents condemn sexual relations between persons of the same sex (91 per cent of the respondents over 60 years old said that homosexual relations were wrong where 56 per cent of the respondents under 24 years of age said the same).
- 41 per cent of the respondents supported the decriminalisation of homosexuality in Cyprus.

It has to be said that the higher the educational qualifications of the respondents the more relaxed their attitudes were found.

Fifthly, the purpose of this thesis was to examine the sexual and cultural identities of Cypriot men resident in London who have sex with men by considering current issues in the sociology of sexuality and ethnic minorities' studies. Further research is needed to try and discuss the link among a series of theoretical debates relating to race,[2] ethnicity and gender. Such research would be concerned generally with the ways that historical events, social relationships, and human action come together to create or construct identities, and with how those identities are reproduced, maintained, and transformed. It would highlight the different ways that the Greek-Cypriot ethnicity is expressed and organised within the British culture and also it would link the cultural, sexual, political and economical facets of ethnicity.[3]

Sixthly, research into what people contribute – sometimes consciously, often unconsciously – to the making of their own identities would shed further light onto the extent to which cultural and structural assimilation takes place among the Greek-Cypriots living in Britain. What are the group assets or characteristics that have implications on the salience of ethnic and racial identities would be the main focus of research. Yinger (1986, p.31) presents us with an 'other things equal' version of the effects of these characteristics and group factors on the salience of ethnic and racial identities that can be used as a guideline when exploring issues of ethnicity and race among the Cypriots living in England.

Lastly, to get a really helpful perspective on the context in which Cypriot gay and bisexual men live, one needs to do a further body of interviewing with Cypriot heterosexual men. In these interviews, the following issues could be addressed: How these men view friendship with other men? What are the emotional and physical boundary markers which distinguish a 'normal' heterosexual friendship, from a friendship which these men would consider inappropriate, unacceptable, or stigmatised?; Which sexual practices [and/or ideas of friendship and love] are in themselves the identifying marks of non-heterosexual commitment?; How far a Cypriot heterosexual man can allow himself physical/genital contact with another man, and still keep his self-image as heterosexual (a) in his own eyes; and (b) in the eyes of his heterosexual peers.

Therefore, by doing such research one could get a good descriptive account of similar processes, issues, practices, role-terms, and experiences. That would enable us to see and understand the range of contrasts, overlaps, and distinctions.

Dichotomies and the Greek Culture

So, to what extent should the members of this research sample of Greek gay men be viewed as having successfully integrated the duality of their experiences as Greek and as gay men into one healthy and positive Greek gay identity? Those prone to respond from a western dominant culture perspective would likely to say that these men do not have an integrated positive Greek gay identity because they are living in dichotomy. Although they may be sharing themselves as gay and even as Greek gay men in the gay community, they have truncated the sharing of themselves as gays with their families and lessened their participation in their Greek communities. In the dominant culture, dichotomy is viewed as antithetical to integration. However, it is important that we also consider the response through a Greek cultural lens. Within a Greek culture, learning to live and solidify one's identity within dichotomy is a normal part of adult development (Fygetakis, 1997).

Moving beyond illustrations from Greek popular culture, Welts (1982) has observed that many first-generation Greek-American children have been thrust into parenting themselves while they are at the same time expected to act as though they are dependent upon their parents. This is particularly apparent in regard to education. As was the case with the members of this research sample, most Greek immigrants have pushed their children to reach higher levels of education than they themselves had been able to achieve. Thus Greek immigrant parents may not be particularly able to understand what their children are learning or to help their children with their homework. Ultimately, the children may be left on their own to make such major decisions as choosing a college or university. Furthermore, some children may serve in the role of language and cultural interpreters for their mothers and grandmothers when they go shopping or to doctor's appointments (Callinicos, 1990).

These illustrations provide a glimpse into the paradoxical cultural structure within which Greeks live. So why should Greek gay men act any less Greek? Holden (1972) says, 'Spirit and flesh, ideal and reality, triumph and despair – you name them and the Greeks suffer or enjoy them as the constant poles of their being, swinging repeatedly from one to the other and back again, often contriving to embrace both poles simultaneously, but above all never reconciled, never contented, never still' (p.27).

Some conclusions can be drawn from the above discussion:

- Because Anglo-Greek gay men have been socialised within this type of family context (as explained above), we would expect them to approach and balance the dichotomies of their reality by exercising behaviours similar to those modelled by their parents.
- Although children are generally expected not to have opinions and to obey parental instruction, they may also be forced by circumstances to assume adult responsibilities and decision-making tasks. As Welts (1982) notes, 'Dutifully, they ignore the contradiction'.
- I would propose that Anglo-Greek gay men are simply being culturally consistent when they stay closeted in Greek community yet visible and active otherwise. Greeks are used to living their lives in dichotomy. This is not to say that Anglo-Greek gay men do not feel the effects of oppression or do not feel pain and regret over such dichotomy.

The Resolution of Role Strain

From the discussion on identity (see Chapters 2 and 3) we may then conclude the following: Structurally, the safest cases are those where (i) no one knows or (ii) everyone – or, at least, everyone who is anyone – knows. These automatically reduce the number of stress-producing situations and the potential for the circulation of knowledge (as opposes to rumour). In the case of partial disclosure, some strategies are more likely to be safe (in the sense that they represent some sort of equilibrium, with relatively little inherent tendency to change) in the long term than others. Compartmentalization is safer if it is complete and if the various clusters are separated by existing social or geographical boundaries. Collusion is more likely to be successful in the long term the fewer the people involved and the closer (more committed) they are to the discloser. The central point is that partial disclosure creates some strain. The better strategies reduce the strain, but in the last analysis the success of any such strategy will depend on the amount of energy, which the individual is willing and able to expend on maintaining that unstable state of affairs.

However, a number of drawbacks may have arisen from the analysis of the 'coming out' concept and the role of disclosure during this book:

Firstly, coming out is a process in more ways than the exposition so far has allowed. Coming out also involves a series of disclosures and accommodations to a new lifestyle, not merely the acquisition of a new and isolated piece of information, however explosive it might be. Coming out is a constant struggle against those who, on the one hand, accept the disclosure and then, on the other, refuse to accept its implications: refusal to accept a lover, etc. The answer is that this does not involve the gay individual in a process of passing. Rather, it involves a battle of wills on a different level, although collusive strategies might well figure.

Secondly, the accounts and analyses given in Chapters 2, 3 and 4 do assume that individuals have effective control over disclosure and this is clearly not always the case. A man prosecuted for cottaging, for example, will, if his name appears in the local press – and this is the real threat of such prosecutions – find his carefully nurtured disclosure network summarily destroyed. Likewise, the practice of 'outing', whether done for salacious motives by the tabloid press or for political considerations by gay groups, deprives the individual of control over disclosure and social identity. The very fact that outing is so controversial underlines the importance that is accorded to this control.

Thirdly, it might have been suggested during my arguments that the individual especially he who engages in the strategy of compartmentalisation, has perfect knowledge of the structure of his network. This is clearly unlikely, especially, as has been noted earlier, in the more distant parts of the friendship network. The better his knowledge of the network, the more likely it is that the strategy will succeed. Indeed, the consequences of getting it wrong may be disastrous. It is for this reason that the individual will, if the model is correct, spend some energy in ensuring that he has got it right. But, even so, the successful compartmentalizer is the one who invokes, in the defence of his secret, entrenched social divisions rather than fluid patterns of mere friendships or gay camaraderie.

Finally, it has been suggested that the process of coming out is not an ineluctable one of psychological necessity, but one that is situated in and influenced by a real and immediate social context. A better understanding of the process and its ramifications that can be gained merely from endless refining of the stages of disclosure is possible if the social strategy is integrated into the process of individual becoming.

The following important conclusions can be drawn from the above discussion:

- A central assumption of traditional accounts of coming out is that sexual identity will become the primary identity: the one around which the individual's life will be arranged and articulated. In this thesis, I have suggested that there will be cases in which this is an impossible or highly unsatisfactory possibility and have suggested ways in which the resulting strains are accommodated and managed. Furthermore, I have suggested that identity is a process of accommodation to a social world, rather than a dominating and pre-disposing psychic force. This perspective allows, far more easily than traditional accounts of self-concept or identity, the possibility

of multiple identities, which compete, collude, and compromise in the process of everyday life.
- The personal accounts that come out of this research reinforced the above argument and also showed that individuals and groups at different places and times construct different identities. For a lot of the Cypriot men resident in London having sex with men the translation of their sexual desires and behaviour into a political statement of a gay identity is not only difficult but may be strongly resisted. They choose to see themselves in terms of other personal relationships with their families, their peers at work and with other members of their community.

Coming Out and Integration

A major part of this book dealt with a wide range of experiences and dilemmas confronting Cypriot gay men living in London. More explicitly it examined issues of ethnicity, culture, and sexual orientation as salient aspects of human identity and attempted to shed some light on these issues and their interactive effects. The major findings are summarised below:

A major difference between English family structures and some ethnic family ones centers on the integration of the extended family within its support system. For the ethnic person the family is the basis of their roots and the focal point of their ethnic identity. 'Coming out' to the family tends to involve both the nuclear and extended family systems. Such a family collective is the major support system for the ethnic persons and is the source of great strength and pride. In other words the family is the emotional bond for the conscious self and personal psychology. For minority gays coming out to the family not only jeopardises the inter-family relationships, but also threatens their strong association with their ethnic community. As a result minority gays may run the risk of feeling uprooted as an ethnic person.

Families and friends of minority gay men can be a source of support. Anxieties about rejection from families and friends may become exaggerated and may lack a realistic perspective. It is important for minority gays to examine the consequences and benefits of coming out to family members on case-by-case basis. A change in the quality of the relationship can be expected upon disclosure. Such change may result in a more intimate and mature relationship. With parents this may mean changing the parent-child role into an adult-adult role where a sense of mutual respect develops.

Within these value systems heterosexual lifestyles are considered to be the norm, and family members are expected to marry and to continue the traditional family system. Gay lifestyles are incongruent with these value systems. Upon disclosing one's sexual identity the family may be faced with a crisis. The challenge for the family centers around its ability to be flexible and to adapt the normative expectations of its members, rather than to be rigid and to reject other lifestyle alternatives that exist within the family. Some families may decide to accept their gay family member's lifestyle including the lover but not discuss the matter. Other families may be more active in discussing the issues in a supportive way. In any case, respect for the beliefs and values of all family members are the basis for maintaining unity in the family.

Garay (1978) proposed that Latino families respond to the coming out process in a manner corresponding to the stages of grief and mourning. The first stage, denial, is the initial reaction of avoiding or denying the emotional contents of the situation. The second stage, reproach, is characterised by anger, mutual accusations and/or some form of aggression. The third stage, compromise, is characterised by seeking a cause for homosexual behaviour in which someone is at fault. The fourth stage, acceptance, is characterised by incorporating the individual and their primary partner into the family unit. This grief process may extend to the issues of AIDS, which complicates the coming out process and may be an unspoken source of anxiety and stress to all family members.

Additionally, this book examined the factors that affect an Anglo-Cypriot individual's choice of identification with Anglo-Cypriots and gay identity. Twenty-two Cypriot men resident in London who have sex with men were interviewed. Results indicated that most of the respondents identified more strongly with their gay identity than with their Anglo-Cypriot identities; however, most indicated that acknowledgment of both aspects of identity was preferred. Other situational factors, including disclosure of gay identity to family and to the Anglo-Cypriot community, as well as discrimination because of sexual orientation, and race, were examined in regard to identity development.

The following additional conclusions were drawn from this analysis:

Firstly, ethnic background is not necessarily a barrier between the gay family member and the parents, even when values, beliefs, and traditions mitigate against the acceptance of homosexuality. The family is considered as a unique, individual unit. The individual must assess the strengths and weaknesses of the family in question before deciding to 'come out' (to his family) and ask a number of questions: What is the quality of the family dynamics? Does this family function well when there is a crisis or conflict?; Do the members communicate effectively?; A foundation of healthy family dynamics is necessary if the outcome of disclosure is to be successful. Furthermore, he needs to ask: How does the family prioritise its values?; is there flexibility in the use and understanding of these values?; what do the family members understand about homosexuality?

Secondly, what are the criteria for a successful outcome with this family? The parents may never approve of the son's sexual orientation. They may only achieve tolerance, not acceptance, and may demand that the son keep his gay life-style separate from family life. Is the individual prepared to compromise?

Thirdly, has the individual lost an important connection with his culture? What are the present and future psychological and practical consequences of this loss? Does the individual have a place among gay peers in which to feel at home?

Sexual Identity Formation for Ethnic Minority Individuals: The Future

Sexual Identity is not an essential fixed given for any individual, nor is it developed within a vacuum. Concepts of lesbian and gay identity have evolved over a two hundred-year span in the West, heavily influenced by social and political conditions, from the initial sexual categories in sexology, to a male homosexual identity, to the New Woman, to lesbians, gays, bisexuals, and most recently 'queer' identity. The modern homosexual identity remains a Western construct. There is no comparable sexual identity in Cypriot culture.

For a Cypriot man in Cyprus to have a gay identity, he has to define himself through Western cultural concepts. For an Anglo-Cypriot who is defining a sexual identity, he or she also must adapt Western codes of sexuality and sexual expression to meet his/her own needs. At the same time, this individual will have to respond to Cypriot cultural influences, which require a different set of demands on family responsibilities, privacy, and the forms of sexual expression that are considered to be acceptable. Weighing the Western pressure to come out and be openly gay against the Cypriot cultural demand for privacy requires a balance among opposing forces. While some individuals may never openly admit or act on their homosexuality, others will embrace the Western model enthusiastically; still others will be openly gay/lesbian only in safe (generally non-Cypriot) environments. However, the Cypriot cultural restrictions on open expression of sexuality may create a diminished dichotomisation of heterosexual versus homosexual behaviour. Given the importance of the concept of having only a private expression of sexuality, there could actually be more allowance of fluidity within a sexual behavioural continuum.

The cultural prohibition against having a definition or declaration of sexual orientation/identity may ironically result in a broader range of acceptable behaviours even as the public identities are more narrowly defined. Social science research on gay and lesbian issues has focused on the evolution of people whose primary political and ethnic identification is as gay or lesbian, and who have been able to organise a multidimensional way of life on the basis of their sexual orientation. But we need to focus on other forms of homosexuality – other ways in which homosexual desire and behaviour have been organised, understood, named, or left deliberately unnamed (Chauncey, 1989). We need to be careful not to view the evolution of a homosexual identity only through a Western lens, expecting that non-Western cultures, with modernisation, will eventually follow the same course in achieving greater openness with homosexual behaviour. Cultural differences in the construction of identity and in the expression of sexuality have to be taken into account. We are just beginning to know which questions to ask.

There is still little empirical information about sexuality, sexual identity, and sexual expression for Anglo-Cypriots and other non-Western ethnic minority groups. Future research questions will address important factors, specific to each cultural group, examining: (1) modes of sexual expression; (2) constructions of sexual identity; (3) attitudes toward sexuality in the context of measuring cultural values and generational differences; (4) assimilation to majority values; (5) gender roles; (6) expectations of one's family of origin; (7) the economic role of the family, particularly for women and immigrants; (8) importance of procreation; (9) ties to the ethnic community; (10) assimilation and acculturation; and (11) the history of discrimination and oppression specific to that cultural group. By exploring sexuality in the context of these factors, the discourse is broadened for all individuals, as silences are broken and the range of sexual expression is more carefully articulated.

Since the issue of sexuality has been so private within many non-Western cultures, there is little knowledge of how ethnic minority individuals, forging identities within a Western culture, experience or express their homosexuality. The expression of sexuality in ethnic minority literature, film, and art gives us some clues, but we also need to study the attitudes and experiences of ethnic minority individuals across the lifespan, from adolescents developing an emergent sexuality to elders reflecting on their personal experiences. The very privateness of the concept of Anglo-Cypriot and other cultural groups about homosexuality has kept us in silence. We are now asking the questions, and it is also up to us to find the answers.

It is my hope that this book has contributed towards a better understanding of the complexities involved for men who identify as Anglo-Greek gays. If there is a main point to be made, it is that these men should not be discounted as simply not brave enough, not proud enough, or not having enough of a positive gay identity.

In the words of Tony:

> My parents, like most of the Greek-Cypriots, think that being gay is an English thing. My culture has to be taught that it's not. It is just a human thing. (Tony)

Notes

1 The first piece of research was conducted in July 1994 by the Centre of Applied Research in Nicosia. The second one was conducted in July 1995 and the third one in June 1997. Each time 600 hundred respondents are randomly selected across all socio-economic strata and interviewed at their homes. The research covered the territory controlled by the Republic of Cyprus. The sample was drawn among Greek-speaking population age 18 and above. The sample was stratified according to sex, district of residence, age group and rural/urban residence.

   The questionnaire covered four major areas of interest:

   • Attitudes on the economy
   • Attitudes on politics and politicians
   • Attitudes on civil rights, personal fears and expectations
   • Attitudes on sexual ethics

   The Centre of Applied Research of Cyprus College represents Cyprus in the International Social Survey Programme. It conducts the 'Cypriot Social Attitudes Survey' annually with the exception of the year 1996.

2. Stuart Hall argues that collective identity and experience are not given but 'are constructed historically, culturally, politically – and the concept which refers to this is 'ethnicity'. The term ethnicity acknowledges the place of history, language and culture in the construction of subjectivity and identity' (1992, p.257).

   Race, in its colloquial usage at least, implies a naturalness that is difficult to overcome. Ethnicity, on the other hand, conveys both this constructed quality – something made by history and culture and therefore variable and changing – and, in its emphasis on self-consciousness, the participation of groups themselves in the construction, reproduction, and transformation of their own identities.
3. F. Anthias's book discusses the Cypriot migration to Britain within the context of New Commonwealth migration as a whole and within current developments in the field of racial and ethnic relations.

Appendix

Section 1
Sections 1–4 to be completed by interviewer

A. SOCIO-ECONOMIC BACKGROUND

1.1 Gender:

1.2 Age last Birthday: _____ Years

1.3 Country of Birth: _____

1.4 Current Nationality (if different): _____

1.5 Ethnicity _____

1.6 Current Place of Residence: _____

1.7 Marital Status
    Single (never married) 0
    Currently married 1
    Divorced 2
    Separated 3
    Widowed 4

1.8 Living arrangements:
    Alone 1
    With parents/relatives 2
    With wife/female partner 3
    With same sex partner (s) 4
    With friends (flat mates) 5
    Other arrangements 6

1.9 Number of children: _____

1.10 Religious Affiliation: _____

1.11 Degree of observation: Very committed indeed 1
                              Quite committed   2
                              Not very committed   3
                              Not at all committed   4

1.12 Highest educational level Secondary   1
                                 University/polytechnic 2
                                 Other higher education 3
                                 Other _____   4

1.13 Age of leaving full time education   _____

Section 2

B.   HOMOSEXUAL IDENTITY (Explain need for comparative sexual data)

2.1 Have you ever had a (heterosexual) girlfriend? If so, how many?

2.2 How old were you when you had (if any) your first ever heterosexual penetrative sexual experience?   _____ years

2.3 Have you ever been engaged? (Why?)

2.4 How would you describe your   Homosexual   1
     sexual orientation now?   Gay   2
                                     Bisexual   3
                                     Other   4
                                     Specify _____
                                     (Use Term)

2.5 At what age did you first think that you might be sexually 'different'?   _____

2.6 At what age did you first define that difference as 'homosexuality'?   _____

2.7 How do you feel about your   Satisfied   1
     (homo)sexuality?   Indifferent/OK 2
                                    Unhappy   3
                                    Depressed   4
                                    Proud   5

2.8	You personally, how did you feel when you discovered for the first time that you were attracted to the same sex?	Surprised Scared Guilty Worried Comfortable Other _____	1 2 3 4 5 6
2.9	How do you feel about your sexual orientation overall?	_____	
2.10	How, if at all, have your feelings changed over the years?	_____	
2.11	Have you accepted your (homo)sexuality?	Yes No	1 2
2.12	If no, why?	Social conditions Psychological reasons Sexual problems Other	1 2 3 4
2.13	Have you ever tried to commit suicide?	Yes No	1 2
2.14	If yes, what was the reason?	Personally, I could not accept my sexuality The people around me could not understand me Other	1 2 3
2.15	If you have experienced any feelings of fear or guilt, how did you overcome them?	By myself With the help of friends With the help of family Counsellor Still having these feelings	1 2 3 4 5

2.16	If you had the choice, would you have chosen to be gay or straight?	Gay Straight	1 2

2.17 Why?
_____

2.18	Do you believe that homosexuality is:	A choice	1
		An expression of love	2
		A sexual orientation	3
		An evil	4
		A sin	5
		A mental disorder	6
		An emotional disorder	4

2.19 How old were you when you had
your first ever gay sexual experience?
('Sexual' is loosely defined here as including
anything from 'deep'
(wet/French) kissing to fucking)   ____ years

(What happened?)
_____

2.20 If differentiate, how old were
you when you had your first 'real'
gay sexual experience?   ____ years

(What happened?)
_____

2.21 How many (homo)sexual partners do
you think that you've had in your
whole lifetime?
(Exclude deep kissing here)
Of these, how many were: Total _____
Regular _____   Casual _____
(Show Card 'A')

2.22	Do you easily find a sexual partner?	Yes No	1 2

2.23 Where do you usually find a sexual partner?	Pubs Clubs Cruising grounds Cottages Saunas Parties Street Classified ads Paying for it	1 2 3 4 5 6 7 8 9
2.24 What do you fear most in seeking a sexual partner?	Rejection STD HIV/AIDS Being caught out Other	1 2 3 4 5
2.25 With regard to the length of your (homo)sexual relationships, how long have your (last three) relationships lasted?	1 _____ 2 _____ 3 _____	
2.26 Have ANY of your relationships lasted more than two months?	_____	
2.27 Have you ever had what you would call a 'serious' (homosexual) boyfriend?	_____	
2.28 Returning to the present now, how many sexual relationships do you have at the moment? (Please show cards 'A' and 'B')	_____	

	Gender	Regular	Casual	Occasional	Length	Monogamous?
P1						
P2						
P3						
P4						
P5						

IF IN A RELATIONSHIP:

2.29	What do you feel most about your partner?	Tenderness	1
		Love	2
		Companionship	3
		Sexual desire	4
		Friendship	5
		Other	6

2.30 Any sexual problems in your current relationship may be attributed to:
- Lack of communication with your lover — 1
- Infrequent sex life — 2
- Other — 3

2.31 Moving on again, have you ever been to a gay pub or club?
- Never — 1
- Once — 2
- < 10 — 3
- > 10 — 4

2.32 In an average month, how often to you go (gay) pubbing/clubbing? _____

2.33 Other gay/lesbian related activities, e.g. sports/outdoor groups etc.? _____

2.34 Do you ever attend gyms, whether or not gay? (Details) _____

Section 3

C. FAMILY LIFE AND FRIENDS

(Are both your parents still alive?) _____

(Are your parents still married?) _____

3.1 Do you have any brothers or sisters? _____

If yes, how many? _____

Appendix

3.2	Does any of your family (of origin) know about your sexual orientation?	Mother only	1
		Father only	2
		Both	3
		Nobody	4
		Everybody	5
		Sibling(s) only	6
		Other	7

3.3	How did your parents react when they found out about your sexuality?	Acceptance	1
		Rejection	2
		Understanding	3
		Support	4

3.4 If married, do your family
(of pro-creation) know
Wife _____   Children _____

3.5	Turning to friends now, how many of your friends know about your sexual orientation? (Card 'C')	All	1
		None	2
		Most	3
		A few	4
		About half	5
		Other	6

3.6 How did each react? (Give a brief description)

3.7	Thinking about your free time now, who do you spend most of your free time mixing with? (Card 'D')	Gay colleagues	1
		Straight colleagues	2
		Gay friends	3
		Straight	4
		No particular group	5
		Other	6

Section 4

D. ETHNIC MINORITIES AND SEXUALITY

4.1 Participation in social or political events in the following communities:
Cypriot-British only
Lesbian/gay only
Both lesbian/gay and Cypriot-British

4.2 In which community do you feel more comfortable?
Lesbian/gay
Cypriot-British
Neither or both

4.3 What do you consider to be your identity?
Anglo-Cypriot gay man?
Gay Anglo-Cypriot?
Neither or both

4.4 Disclosure of gay identity to family:
Yes
No
Disclosure of gay identity to parents:
Yes
No
Disclosure of gay identity to friends:

4.5 Easier or harder to 'come out' to Anglo-Cypriots?
Easier
Harder
No difference

4.6 Feel acknowledged and accepted in gay community?
Yes
No
Unsure

4.7 Experienced discrimination because of being Cypriot?
Experienced discrimination because of being gay?
Experienced more discrimination because of being both Cypriot and gay?

Bibliography

Allen, P.G. (1984), 'Beloved Women: The Lesbian in American Indian Culture', in T. Darty and S. Potter (eds), *Women Identified Women*, Palo Alto, CA: Mayfield.
Amaro, H. (1988), *Coming Out: Hispanic Lesbians, their Families and Communities*, Paper presented at the National Coalition of Hispanic Mental Health and Human Services Organisation, Austin, Texas.
Anthias F. (1992), *Ethnicity, Class, Gender and Migration*, London: Avebury.
Atchley, R.C. (1982), 'The Aging Self', *Psychotherapy: Theory, Research, and Practice*, 19(4), pp.388–96.
Atkinson, D., Morton, G. and Sue, D. (1979), *Counselling American Minorities*, Dubuque, IA: William C. Brown.
Becker, H. (1963), *Outsiders*, New York: Free Press.
Bell, A.P. and Weinberg, M.S. (1975) (1978), *Homosexualities*, London: Mitchell Beazley.
Blumstein P.W. and Schwartz, P. (1975), 'Lesbianism and Bisexuality', in Erich Goode and Richard Troiden (eds), *Sexual Deviance and Sexual Deviants*, New York: William Morrow.
Blumstein P.W. and Schwartz, P. (1977), 'Bisexuality: Some Social Psychological Issues', *Journal of Social Issues*, 33(2), pp.30–45.
Brannen, J. (1988), 'Research Note: The Study of Sensitive Subjects', *Sociological Review*, vol. 36, pp.552–63.
Bucuvalas, E.G., Lavrakas, C.G. and Stamatos, P.G. (1980), *Treasured Greek Proverbs: The Greeks have a Saying for it ...*, Ridgewood, NJ: Treasured Greek Proverbs.
Burgess, R.G. (1982), 'The Unstructured Interview as Conversation', in Robert Burgess (ed.), *Field Research: A Source Book and Field Manual*, London: Unwin and Hyman.
Caplan, P. (1989), *The Cultural Construction of Sexuality*, London: Routledge.
Carballo-Diequez, A. (1989), 'Hispanic Culture, Gay Male Culture, and AIDS: Counselling Implications', *Journal of Councelling and Development*, 68, pp.26–30.
Carrier, J.M. (1976), 'Family Attitudes and Mexican Male Homosexuality', *Urban Life*, 5(3), pp.359–75.
Carrier, J.M. (1977), '"Sex-role Preference" as an Explanatory Variable in Gay Behaviour', *Achives of Sexual Behaviour*, 6(1), pp.53–65.

Carrier, J.M. (1985), 'Mexican Male Bisexuality', in F. Klein and T. Wolf (eds), *Bisexualities: Theory and Research*, New York: The Haworth Press.

Carrier, J.M. (1989a), 'Gay Liberation and Coming Out in Mexico', *Journal of Homosexuality*, 17(3–4), pp.225–52.

Carrier, J.M. (1989b), 'Sexual Behaviour and Spread of AIDS in Mexico', *Medical Anthropology*, 10, pp.129–42.

Cass, V.C. (1979), 'Homosexual Identity Formation: A Theoretical Model', *Journal of Homosexuality*, 4 (3), pp.219–35.

Casson, R.W. (1981), *Language, Culture and Cognition: Anthropological Perspectives*, New York: Macmillan Publishing Co. Inc.

Chan, C. (1992), 'Cultural Considerations in Counselling Asian American Lesbians and Gay Men', in S. Dworkin and F. Gutierrez (eds), *Counselling Gay Men and Lesbians*, Alexandria, VA: American Association for Counselling and Development.

Colman, E. (1982), 'Developmental Stages of the Coming-Out Process', in William Paul et al. (eds), *Homosexuality: Social, Psychological, and Biological Issues*, Beverly Hills: Sage.

Connell, R.W. (1987), *Gender and Power*, Cambridge: Polity Press.

Connell, R.W. (1995), *Masculinities*, Cambridge: Polity Press.

Cory, D. and LeRoy, J. (1963), *The Homosexual and His Society a View From Within*, New York: Citadel Press.

Coxon, A.P.M. (1992), 'Strategies in Eliciting Sensitive, Sexual Information: The case of Gay Men', *Project SIGMA*, working paper no.25, Southbank Polytechnic, London.

Daniel, H. and Parker, R. (1993), *Sexuality, Politics and AIDS in Brazil in Another World?*, London: Falmer Press.

Dank, B.M. (1985), 'Coming Out in the Gay World', *Psychiatry*, 34, pp.180–97.

Davies, P.M. (1983), *The Control of Disclosure*, PhD thesis, Faculty of Economic and Social Studies, University College, Cardiff.

Davies, P.M. (1992), 'The Role of Disclosure in Coming Out Among Gay Men', in K. Plummer (ed.), *Modern Homosexualities: Fragments of Lesbian and Gay Experience*, London: Routledge.

Davis, J. (1997), *People of the Mediterranean*, London: Routledge.

De Monteflores, C. (1989), 'Notes on the Management of Difference', in T.S. Stein and C.J. Cohen (eds), *Contemporary Perspectives on Psychotherapy with Lesbians and Gay Men*, New York: Plenum.

De Monteflores, C. and Schultz, S.J. (1978), 'Coming Out: Similarities and Differences for Lesbians and Gay Men', *Journal of Social Issues*, 34(3), pp.59–72.

DuBay, W.H. (1987), *Gay Identity: The Self Under Ban*, Jefferson: McFarland and Co.

Du Boulay, J. (1974), *Portrait of a Greek Mountain Village*, London: Oxford University Press.

Dubisch, J. (ed.) (1986), *Gender and Power in Rural Greece*, New Jersey: Princeton University Press.

Dyne, L. (1980), 'Is D.C. becoming the gay capitol of America', *Washingtonian*, September, pp.96–101, 133–41.

Espin, O. (1984), 'Cultural and Historical Influences on Sexuality in Hispanic/Latina Women: Implications for psychotherapy', in C. Vance (ed.), *Pleasure and Danger: Exploring Female Sexuality*, London: Routledge and Kegan Paul.

Espin, O. (1987), 'Issues of Identity in the Psychology of Latina Lesbians', in Boston Lesbian Psychologies Collective (eds), *Lesbian Psychologies*, Urbana and Chicago, IL: University of Illinois Press.

Faubion, J.D. (1993), *Modern Greek Lessons*, Princeton, NY: Princeton University Press.

Foucault, M. (1980), *The History of Sexuality. Volume 1: An Introduction*, New York: Vintage.

Fygetakis, M.L. (1997), 'Greek American Lesbians: Identity Odysseys of Honorable Good Girls', in B. Green (ed.), *Ethnic and Cultural Diversity among Lesbians and Gay Men*, Thousand Oaks, California: Sage.

Gagnon, J.H. and Simon, W.S. (eds) (1967), *Sexual Deviance*, London: Harper and Row.

Gallop, J. (1982), *Feminism and Psychoanalysis: The Daughter's Seduction*, London: Macmillan.

Garnets, L. and Kimmel, D. (1991), 'Lesbian and Gay Male Dimensions in the Psychological Study of Human Diversity', in J. Goodchilds (ed.), *Psychological Perspectives on Human Diversity in America*, Washington, DC: American Psychological Association.

Georgiou, G.J. and Veresies, K. (1991), *The Knowledge, Attitudes, Beliefs and Practices Survey of 15–18 year old Cypriot Schoolchildren Regarding AIDS*, Geneva: World Health Organisation.

Glasser, B.G. and Strauss, A.L. (1967), *The Discovery of Grounded Theory: Strategies for Qualitative Research*, Chicago: Aldine Press.

Gock, T.S. (1992), 'Asian-Pacific Islander Issues: Identity Integration and Pride', in B. Berzon (ed.), *Positively Gay*, Berkley, CA: Celestial Arts.

Goddard, V. (1989), 'Honour and Shame: the Control of Women's Sexuality and Group Identity in Naples', in P. Caplan (ed.), *The Cultural Construction of Sexuality*, London: Routledge.

Goffman, E. (1963), *Stigma; Notes on the Management of Spoiled Identity*, Harmondsworth: Penguin.

Greene, B. (1986), 'When the Therapist is White and the Patient is Black: Considerations for psychotherapy in the Feminist Heterosexual and Lesbian Communities', *Women and Therapy*, 5, pp.41–66.

Greene, B. (1993), 'Psychotherapy with African-American Women: Integrating Feminist and Psychodynamic Models', *Journal of Training and Practice in Professional Psychology*, 7(1), pp.49–66.

Greene, B. (1994), 'Ethnic Minority Lesbians and Gay Men: Mental Health and

Treatment Issues', *Journal of Consulting and Clinical Psychology*, 62(2).
Gutierrez, F. and Dworkin, S. (1992), 'Gay, Lesbian, and African American: Managing the Integration of Identities', in S. Dworkin and F. Gutierrez (eds), *Counselling Gay Men and Lesbians*, Alexandria, VA: American Association of Councelling and Development.
Hammersmith, S.K. and Weinberg, M.S. (1973), 'Homosexual Identity: Commitment, Adjustment, and Significant Others', *Sociometry*, 36, pp.56–79.
Hencken, J.D. (1984), 'Conceptualisations of Homosexual Behaviour Which Preclude Homosexual Self-labelling', in John P. DeCecco (ed.), *Bisexual and Homosexual Identities: Critical Clinical Issues*, New York: The Haworth Press.
Hendin, H. (1969), *Black Suicide*, New York: Basic Books.
Herdt, G. (1981), *Guardians of the Flutes: Idioms of Masculinity*, New York: McGraw Hill.
Herzfeld, M. (1980), 'Honour and Shame: Problems in the Comparative Analysis of Moral Systems', *Man* (n.s.), Vol. 15, pp. 339–51.
Hidalgo, H. (1984), 'The Puerto Rican Lesbian in the United States', in T. Darty and S. Porter (eds), *Women Identified Women*, Palo Alto, CA: Mayfield.
Hidalgo, H. and Hidalgo-Christensen, E. (1976), 'The Puerto-Rican Lesbian and the Puerto-Rican Community', *Journal of Homosexuality*, 2, pp.109–21.
Hill, I. (1987), *The Bisexual Spouse: Different Dimensions in Human Sexuality*, VA: Barlina Books.
Hirschon, R. (1989), *Heirs of the Greek Catastrophe: the Social Life of Asia Minor Refugees in Piraeus*, Oxford: Oxford University Press.
Holden, D. (1972), *Greece without Columns: The Making of the Modern Greeks*, Philadelphia: J.B. Lippincott.
Humphreys, L. (1970), *Tearoom Trade*, London: Duckworth.
Icard, L. (1986), 'Black Gay Men and Conflicting Social Identities: Sexual Orientation Versus Racial Identity', *Journal of Social Work and Human Sexuality*, 4(1/2), pp.83–93.
Kalton, G. (1993), 'Sampling Considerations in Research on HIV Risk and Illness', in D.G. Ostrow and R.C. Kessler (eds), *Methodological Issues in Aids Behavioral Research*, New York: Plenum Press.
Kinsey, A. (1948), *Sexual Behaviour in the Human Male*, Philadelphia: Saunders.
Lemert, E.M. (1951), *Social Pathology*, New York: McGraw Hill.
Loftus, E. and Palmer, R.L. (1974), 'Reconstruction of Automobile Destruction: An Example of the Interaction Between Language and Memory', *Journal of Verbal Learning and Verbal Behaviour*, 13, pp.585–9.
Loizos, P. and Papataxiarchis, E. (1991), 'Gender, Sexuality and the Person in Greek Culture', in P. Loizos and E. Papataxiarchis (eds), *Contested Identities: Gender and Kinship in Modern Greece*, New Jersey: Princeton University Press.
MacDonald, A. (1984), 'Bisexuality: Some Comments on Research and Theory', *Journal of Homosexuality*, 6(3), pp.21–36.
Marshall, G. (1981), 'Accounting for Deviance', *The International Journal of*

Sociology and Social Policy, vol. 1, no. 1.

Mays, V. and Cochran, S. (1988), 'The Black Women's Relationship Project: A National Survey of Black Lesbians', in M. Shernoff and W. Scott (eds), *The Sourcebook on Lesbian/Gay Health Care*, Washington, DC: National Lesbian and Gay Health Foundation.

McIntosh, M. (1968), 'The Homosexual Role', *Social Problems*, 16, pp.182–92.

McWhirter, D.P. and Mattison, A.M. (1984), *The Male Couple*, Englewood Cliffs, NJ: Prentice-Hall.

Mead, M. (1928), *The Coming of Age in Samoa*, New York: William Morrow.

Merton, R.K. (1949), *Social Theory and Social Structure: Toward the Codification of Theory and Research*, Glencoe, IL: The Free Press.

Mills, C.W. (1974), 'Situated Actions and Vocabularies of Motive', *Power, Politics and People*, London: Oxford University Press.

Minton, H.L. and McDonald, G.J. (1984), 'Homosexual Identity Formation as a Developmental Process', in John P. DeCecco (ed.), *Bisexual and Homosexual Identities: Critical Clinical Issues*, New York: The Haworth Press.

Morales, E. (1983), *Third Word Gays and Lesbians. A Process of Multiple Identities*, Paper presented at the 91st National Convention of the American Psychological Association, Anaheim, California.

Morales, E. (1989), 'Ethnic Minority Families and Minority Gays and Lesbians', *Marriage and Family Review*, 14(3/4), pp.217–39.

Morales, E. (1990), 'Ethnic Minority Families and Minority Gays and Lesbians', in F. Bozett and M. Sussman (eds), *Homosexuality and Family Relations*, New York: The Haworth Press.

Moses, A.E. and Hawkins, R. (1982), *Counselling Lesbian Women and Gay Men: A Life Issues Approach*, St Louis, MO: C.V. Mosby.

Padgug, R. (1989), 'Sexual Matters: Rethinking Sexuality in History', in Duberman, Vicinus and Chauncey (eds), *Hidden from History: Reclaiming the Lesbian and Gay Past*, London: Penguin Books.

Paul, J. (1984), 'The Bisexual Identity: An Idea Without Social Recognition', *Journal of Homosexuality*, 9 (2/3), pp.45–64.

Piaget, J. (1962), *Plays, Dreams and Imitation in Childhood*, New York: Norton.

Pitt-Rivers, J. (1965), 'Honour and Social Status', in J.G. Peristiany (ed.), *Honour and Shame: the Values of Mediterranean Society*, London: Weidenfeld and Nocholson.

Plummer, K. (1975), *Sexual Stigma*, London: RKP.

Plummer, K. (1981a), 'Sexual Categories: Some Research Problems in the Labelling Perspective of Homosexuality' and 'Building a Sociology of Homosexuality', in Kenneth Plummer (ed.), *The Making of the Modern Homosexual*, London: Hutchinson.

Plummer, K. (1981b), 'Going Gay: Identities, Life Cycles and Lifestyles in the Male Gay World', in J. Hart and D. Richardson (eds), *The Theory and Practice of Homosexuality*, London: RKP.

Plummer, K. (1988), 'The Problem of Patriarchal Masculinities', in *Family, Gender and Welfare*, Milton Keynes: The Open University.
Pomeroy, W.B. et al. (1982), *Taking a Sex History*, New York: Free Press.
Ponse, B. (1978), *Identities in the Lesbian Word: The Social Construction of Self*, Westport, CT: Greenwood Press.
Reber, A.S. (ed.) (1985), *Dictionary of Psychology*, Harmondsworth: Penguin.
Reiss, A.J. Jr (1961), 'The Social Integration of Queers and Peers', *Social Problems*, 9(2), pp.102–20.
Segal, L. (1990), *Slow Motion: Changing Masculinities, Changing Men*, London: Virago Press.
Sophie, J. (1986), 'A Critical Examination of Stage Theories of Lesbian Identity Development', *Journal of Homosexuality*, 12(2), pp.39–51.
Stonequist, E.V. (1961), *The Marginal Man*, New York: Russell and Russell.
Strauss, A.L. (1987), *Qualitative Analysis for Social Scientists*, Cambridge: Cambridge University Press.
Sykes, G.M. and Matza, D. (1957), 'Techniques of Neutralisation: A Theory of Delinquency', *American Sociological Review*, 22, pp.664–70.
Tapinc, H. (1992), 'Masculinity, Feminity, and Turkish Male Homosexuality', in Kenneth Plummer (ed.), *Modern Homosexualities. Fragments of Lesbian and Gay Experience*, London: Routledge.
Tremble, B., Schneider, M. and Appathurai, C. (1989), 'Growing up Gay or Lesbian in a Multicultural Context', *Journal of Homosexuality*, 17, pp. 253–67.
Troiden, R.R. (1979), 'Becoming Homosexual: A Model of Gay Identity Acquisition', *Psychiatry*, 42, pp.362–73.
Troiden, R.R. (1988), *Gay and Lesbian Identity*, New York: General Hall.
Trumbach, R. (1977), 'London's Sodomites: Homosexual Behaviour in the Eighteenth Century', *Journal of Social History*, 11, pp.1–33.
Vasquez, E. (1979), 'Homosexuality in the Context of the Mexican-American Culture', in D. Kukel (ed.), *Sexual Issues in Social Work: Emerging Concerns in Education and Practice*, Honolulu: University of Hawaii School of Social Work.
Watney, S. (1993), 'Emergent Sexual Identities and HIV/AIDS', in P. Aggleton et al. (eds), *AIDS: Facing the Second Decade*, London: Falmer Press.
Weeks, J. (1985), *Sexuality and its Discontents: Meanings, Myths and Modern Sexualities*, London: RKP.
Weeks, J. (1986), *Sexuality*, London: Tavistock.
Weeks, J. (1989), 'AIDS, Altruism, and the New Right', in E. Carter and S. Watney (ed.), *Taking Liberties AIDS and Cultural Politics*, London: Serpent's Tail.
Weinberg, M.S. and Williams, C.J. (1972), 'Fieldwork Among Deviants: Social Relations With Subjects and Others', in J.D. Douglas (ed.), *Research on Deviance*, New York: Random House.
Weinberg M.S. and Williams, C.J. (1974), *Male Homosexuals: Their Problems and Adaptations*, New York: Penguin.

Weinberg, T.S. (1978), 'On "Doing" and "Being" Gay: Sexual Behaviour and Homosexual Male Self-Identity', *Journal Of Homosexuality*, 4(2), pp.143–56.

Weinberg, T.S. (1983), *Gay Men, Gay Selves: The Social Construction of Homosexual Identities*, New York: Irvington Press.

Welts, E.P. (1982), 'Greek Families', in M. McGoldrick, J.K. Pierce and J. Giordano (eds), *Ethnicity and Family Therapy*, New York: Gildford.

Index

Page numbers in *italics* refer to notes.

acceptance of gayness 18-19
  Cypriot cultural factors 95-101
  see also coming out
activity and passivity, notion of 61-2
alcoholic amnesia 16
allegiance
  conflicts in 51-2
  established priorities in 52-3
Alonso, A.M. and Koreck, M.T. 8
ambivalence 27-9
andras 59, 60-1
Anglo-Cypriots 1, 7, 9, 46
  gay 10, 64-5, 91-114, 106-7
Anthias, F. 1, 6, *11*, *12*, 65, *124*
anti-homosexual backlash 34-5
anti-homosexuality laws 5-6
army recruitment 60-1, *69*
articulation and awareness,
  synergistic 49-50
assimilation 45, 46, 110-11
assimilationist model 41
  collapse of, and search for
  alternative 41-2
Atkinson, D., Morton, G. and Sue,
  D. 47-50, 53
avoidance of homosexual role 15-17,
  21, 22

backlash against homosexuality 34-5
Bell, A.P. and Weinberg, M.S. 33
Bell, A.P., Weinberg, M.S. and
  Hammersmith, S.K. 20
bicultural identity 7
bisexuality 17, 81
  vs homosexuality 50-1
Blumstein, P.W. and Schwartz, P.
  17, 19
Britain *see* Anglo-Cypriots;
  immigration
British culture 116
Bucuvalas, E.G., Lavrakas, C.G. and
  Stamatos, P.G. 100
bullying 22, 108

Carrier, J.M. 54
Cass, V.C. 17, 19, 24, 35, 114
childhood, isolation in 22-3
choice of community 104-6
Christian religion 21, 65-8
CLGG *see* Cypriot Lesbian and Gay
  Group (CLGG)
collusion 33, 118
  within family 99-101
coming out 1-2, 24-5
  choice of community 104-6, 112
  defined 34
  in the family 34-5, 92-5, 112, 120-1
  and integration 120-1
  patterns 113
  resolution of role strain 118-20
  see also acceptance of gayness

commitment 24-5
commonalities, researcher and
   subject 78-80
   perception of 81-2
community/communities
   choice of 104-6, 112
   denial of homosexuality 56
   integrating various 53
   mores 9
   three different 3, 103-8
compartition/compartmentalisation
   32-3, 118, 119
'Completely Drunk' Syndrome 16
conflicts
   in allegiance 51-2
   denial of 50-1
conformity 47-8
constructionist model of sexual
   identity 18-19
control of information disclosure 29-33
counterfeit roles 29-30
covering 31
Cypriot culture
   criticism of 79
   dichotomies and 117-18
   factors in acceptance of gayness
      95-101
   homosexuality in 5-6, 61-3
   sexuality in 58-63
   women in 59-60, 69, 96-8, 99
Cypriot heterosexual men 177
Cypriot Lesbian and Gay Group
   (CLGG) 10, 113
Cyprus
   Island of Love 1, *11*
   social attitudes survey 63-4,
      69-70, 123-4

Davies, P.M. 32-3, 85, 92
denial

   of conflicts 50-1
   of homosexuality 56
deprogramming 17
'deviant' behaviour 15
dichotomies and Greek culture
   117-18
differences
   between researcher and subject
      80-2
   cultural attitudes to sexual
      behaviour 4-5, 8
disavowel 30-1
disclosure *see* coming out; control of
   information disclosure; self-
   disclosure of researcher
'discreditable'/'discredited' identity
   3-4, 29, 43
discrimination 107-8, 112
dissonance 48
double life syndrome 10, 34, 101-2
   effects 108-11, 112-13
   see also multiple identities
double minority status 107-8
Du Boulay, J. 59-60, 61, 99
DuBay, W.H. 14
Dubisch, J. 96-7, 98

effeminate men 15, 62
'escapism' 21
Espin, O. 46-7, 54
established priorities in allegiance
   52-3
ethnic identity
   and queer theory 37-8
   vs sexual identity 7-8
ethnic minorities 47-50, 103-4
ethnic minority gay men 50-3
   Anglo-Cypriot 10, 64-5, 91-114,
      106-7
   psychosocial factors 53-5
   white gay men and 103-4

ethnic minority gay studies 3-5
  future of 122-3
'exploiting' respondents 75

family/families 9, 56
  collusion within 99-101
  coming out in 34-5, 92-5, 112, 120-1
  dichotomies and Greek culture 117-18
  double life syndrome 101-2
  gender roles 95-8
  see also honour
Faubion, J.D. 58, 59, 63
Foucault, M. 3, 18, 57, 58, 59, 61

Gage, N. 96, 98, 99
Gagnon, J.H. and Simon, W.S. 34, 57
Gallop, J. 14
gay Anglo-Cypriots 10, 64-5, 91-114, 106-7
gay bars 23-4
gay community, mainstream 55
gay and lesbian communities, social differences within 36
gay and lesbian studies
  developments in 2-3
  ethnic minorities 3-5
Gay Liberation Movement 6, *12*
gender roles 54
  family 95-8
Georgiou, G.J. 65-6
Goffman, E. 3-4, 27-8, 29, 31, 32
Greek history, homosexuality in 61
Greek-Cypriot culture *see* Cypriot culture
Greene, B. 55, 103

Hencken, J.D. 15-16
Herzfeld, M. 60, 61, 62, *69*

heterosexual courting/marriage 30, 66
heterosexual men 177
'hidden populations' 77, 82-3, 84, *90*
Hirschom, R. 59
history of homosexuality 2-3, *11-12*, 18, 39-41
  Greek 61
Holden, D. 118
homophobic attitudes 3, 31, 54
homosexuality
  in Cypriot culture 5-6, 61-3
  discrimination 107-8, 112
  history of 2-3, *11-12*, 18, 39-41, 61
  role acceptance 18-19, 95-101
  role avoidance 15-17, 21, 22
honour
  appearance of 99, 100
  philotimo 98, 99, 105-6
  and shame value system 59-60, 98-9
host culture 5

identity assumption 23-4
identity components 36-7
identity confusion 20-3
identity, defined 14
identity formation
  ethnic minority gay men 50-3
  minority persons 46-50
  models 18-25
    critique 25-7
  non-heterosexual 14-35
identity as minority 3-4
immersion, resistance and 48
immigration
  assimilationist model 41-2
  into Britain 4, 8-9, *11*, *124*
  sample population 117-18
  see also entries beginning ethnic

information disclosure, control of
    29-33
integration
    and coming out 120-1
    various communities 53
'intermediary' role 45, 46
interviewee profiles *89*
interviewer
    impact of interviews on 82
    -interviewee relationship 77-82
    'interviewer effect' 74
    self-disclosure of 76, *90*
interviews
    planning 73-6
    schedule of sources *88*
    setting 76-7
introspection 48-9
Isherwood, C. 28-9
Island of Love 1, *11*
isolation *see* marginality

just feeling horny 16
just a phase 16

Kalton, G. 83
'keeping mum' 30, 102
Kinsey, A. 18, 40, 75

language 78-9
Loizos, P. 57, 60, 97, 98
Loizos, P. and Papataxiarchis, E.
    62-3
lying 99

McIntosh, M. 15, 18
McWhirter, D.P. and Mattison, A.M.
    25
magazines 23
mainstream gay community 55
maladjustment/adjustment roles
    43-4, 45

'malakras' 62-3, *69*
marginality 39-43
    in childhood 22-3
    concept of 40-1
    feelings of 26, 55, 56
    life-cycle 42-3
    personality traits 43-6
marriage, heterosexual 30, 66
meetings/contacts 23-4
mental health 111, 113
'militancy' 44
minority persons 3-4, 46-50, 107-8
    see also marginality; *entries*
        beginning ethnic
money, sex for 16
Morales, E. 8, 46, 47, 50-3, 54, 55
multiple identities 40-1, 47, 52
    gay Greek-Cypriots 64-5
    negotiation between two worlds
        101-2, 112
    role strain, resolution of 118-20
    see also double life syndrome

'nationalist' roles 45, 46
negotiation between two worlds
    101-2, 112
non-Greek partners 110-11
non-heterosexual identity
    formulation of 14-35
    see also bisexuality;
        homosexuality; *and entries*
        beginning gay
non-probability techniques 84-5

Omofilofilia 6, *12*, 63-4, *69*
ostracism 56
outcast status 56

Park, R. 40-1
partners 109
    non-Greek 110-11

passivity 62-3
  notion of activity and 61-2
Patsalidhou, N. 63-4
personality traits 43-6
philotimo 98, 99, 105-6
place of work 23
Plummer, K. 18, 19, 34, 35
Pomeroy, W.B. et al. 75
'poushtis' 62-3
priests 66, 67, *70-1*
probability sampling 83
processual cycle model 26-7
Project SIGMA 73-4, 77, *86-7*
psema 99
psychiatric model 40
psychosocial factors 53-5

queer theory 35-8
  and ethnic identity 37-8
questionnaires 125-32
  results 111-13
  'self-complete' 74-5

race 116, *124*
race relations cycle 41
racial discrimination 107-8, 112
racist attitudes 3, 80
random walk strategy 84
rare populations 82-3, *90*
Reber, A.S. 14
religion, Christian 21, 65-8
remoteness 31-2
'repair' 21
research issues 91
  future 122-3
research population 10, *12*
  profiles *89*
  sampling 75-6
research project
  aims 7-10, 73
  beginning 6

methodological issues 73-90
  critique 115-17
  see also interviews;
    questionnaires
researcher *see* inteviewer
resistance and immersion 48
resolution of role strain 118-20

sampling
  issues 82-5, 115-17
  methods 75-6, *87-8*
seduction 16
Segal, L. 28
self
  '-indication' and '-reaction' 18
  'ideal' and 'real' 16-17
self-definition of identity 106-7
self-disclosure of researcher 76, *90*
self-esteem 43
semi-structured interviews 74-5
sensitisation 19-20, 26
'sensitive interviews' 74
sex for money 16
sex as power 97
sexual behaviour
  different cultural attitudes to 4-5,
    8
  social values and expectations
    9-10
sexual identity
  defined 14
  theoretical models 18-27
  vs ethnic identity 7-8
sexuality in Cypriot culture 58-63
shame *see* honour
situational homosexuality 16
snowball sampling 76, 83-4
social attitudes survey, Cyprus 63-4,
  69-70, *123-4*
social differences, within gay and
  lesbian communities 36

social models 40-3
social networks 10
social values and expectations 9-10
'stage theory' models, limitations of 25-6
stigma
  effeminate men 62
  'hidden populations' 82-3
  management of 27-33
Stonequist, EV 40-1, 42, 43-4, 45-6
synergistic articulation and awareness 49-50

tape-recorded interviews 73, 76, 85-6

Tapinc, H. 61-2
Tremble, B., Schneider, M. and Appathurai, C. 92
Troiden, R.R. 14, 19-21, 24, 25, 26-7, 53

Weeks, J. 3, 14, 18, 19, 57
Weinberg, M.S. 15, 19
Weinberg, M.S. and Williams, C.J. 40
Welts, E.P. 92, 96, 117, 118
white and ethnic gay men 103-4
women, in Cypriot culture 59-60, *69*, 96-8, 99